# PACIFIC COAST HIGHWAY ROAD GUIDE

Eric J. Bunch

Without the publisher's prior written consent, no part of this book may be copied or communicated electronically or mechanically, including by photocopying, recording or information storage and retrieval systems.
Copyright©2024 Eric J. Bunch

# TABLE OF CONTENTS

## CHAPTER 1: INTRODUCTION TO THE PACIFIC COAST HIGHWAY

- Overview of the Pacific Coast Highway
- History and Significance
- Planning Your Trip: What to Know Before You Go
- Best Times to Travel
- Essential Packing List

## CHAPTER 2: SAN FRANCISCO: THE STARTING POINT

- Iconic Landmarks: Golden Gate Bridge, Alcatraz Island
- Best Neighbourhoods: Fisherman's Wharf, Chinatown, Mission District
- Dining and Accommodation Recommendations
- Day Trips and Nearby Attractions

**CHAPTER 3:** SAN FRANCISCO TO SANTA CRUZ

- Highlights of the Route: Pacifica, Half Moon Bay
- Exploring Santa Cruz: Boardwalk, Surfing Spots
- Natural Wonders: Big Basin Redwoods State Park
- Where to Eat and Stay in Santa Cruz

**CHAPTER 4:** SANTA CRUZ TO MONTEREY

- Scenic Stops: Davenport, Pigeon Point Lighthouse
- Exploring Monterey: Cannery Row, Monterey Bay Aquarium
- 17-Mile Drive: Pebble Beach and Scenic Vistas
- Dining and Accommodation in Monterey

**CHAPTER 5:** MONTEREY TO BIG SUR

- The Beauty of Big Sur: Bixby Creek Bridge, McWay Falls
- Outdoor Activities: Hiking Trails, Pfeiffer Beach
- Iconic Stops: Point Lobos State Natural Reserve, Julia Pfeiffer Burns State Park
- Places to Eat and Stay in Big Sur

## CHAPTER 6: BIG SUR TO SAN LUIS OBISPO

- Rugged Coastlines: Ragged Point, Elephant Seal Rookery
- Historical Sites: Hearst Castle
- Exploring San Luis Obispo: Mission San Luis Obispo, Downtown SLO
- Dining and Accommodation in San Luis Obispo

## CHAPTER 7: SAN LUIS OBISPO TO SANTA BARBARA

- Scenic Villages: Pismo Beach, Avila Beach
- Wine Country: Edna Valley, Paso Robles

- Exploring Santa Barbara: Stearns Wharf, Santa Barbara Mission
- Where to Eat and Stay in Santa Barbara

**CHAPTER 8:** SANTA BARBARA TO LOS ANGELES

- Coastal Gems: Ventura, Malibu
- Iconic LA Landmarks: Santa Monica Pier, Venice Beach, Hollywood
- Best Neighbourhoods: Beverly Hills, Downtown LA, Griffith Park
- Dining and Accommodation in Los Angeles

**CHAPTER 9:** LOS ANGELES TO ORANGE COUNTY

- The OC Beaches: Huntington Beach, Newport Beach, Laguna Beach
- Family Attractions: Disneyland, Knott's Berry Farm
- Dining and Shopping in Orange County
- Accommodation Options in Orange County

**CHAPTER 10:** ORANGE COUNTY TO SAN DIEGO

- Coastal Beauty: San Clemente, Oceanside
- Exploring San Diego: Gaslamp Quarter, Balboa Park, San Diego Zoo
- Best Beaches: La Jolla, Coronado
- Dining and Accommodation in San Diego

**CHAPTER 11:** MAPS

# CHAPTER 1

## INTRODUCTION TO THE PACIFIC COAST HIGHWAY

The Pacific Coast Highway (PCH), commonly known as California State Route 1, is one of the most famous and picturesque roads in the United States. It stretches for almost 650 miles along California's coast, providing stunning vistas of the Pacific Ocean, majestic cliffs, tranquil beaches, and lovely coastal communities. From its southern endpoint in Dana Point, Orange County, to its northern terminus at Leggett, Mendocino County, the PCH offers an incredible experience that draws millions of visitors each year.

The Pacific Coast Highway is more than simply a route; it's a trip across varied landscapes and civilizations. Driving along the route, you will travel through bustling cities like Los Angeles and San Francisco, gorgeous villages like

Carmel-by-the-Sea and Mendocino, and natural treasures like Big Sur, Point Reyes National Seashore, and the Redwood National and State Park. Each section of the highway provides unique experiences and breathtaking views, making it a popular route for road trippers, motorcyclists, and cyclists alike.

One of the most popular sections of the PCH is the trip through Big Sur, where the roadway clings to cliffs above the thundering waves of the Pacific Ocean. This section of the road is well-known for its spectacular landscape, which has been used in numerous films, television shows, and ads. Other significant attractions include the Golden Gate Bridge near San Francisco, the charming community of Sausalito, the historic Hearst Castle in San Simeon, and Malibu's calm beaches.

The PCH also serves as a gateway to several state parks and leisure places. Visitors may stroll the sandy beaches of Huntington Beach, climb the trails of Julia Pfeiffer Burns State Park, and marvel at the towering trees of Humboldt Redwoods State Park. Wildlife aficionados can witness sea lions, elephant seals, and migrating whales along the shore, while birdwatchers can see a variety of seabirds and raptors.

## History and Significance

The Pacific Coast Highway has a rich and varied history, much like the scenery it passes through. The route originated in the early twentieth century when vehicle usage skyrocketed and the need for improved roads became obvious. The concept of a coastal highway connecting the various small villages and growing cities along California's coast was originally proposed in the 1910s. The idea was to build a gorgeous road that would encourage tourism while also serving as an essential transit link for the developing state.

Construction of the PCH began in earnest in the 1920s, with separate pieces completed independently by different counties. The most difficult and famous segment of the roadway, through Big Sur, was built from 1934 to 1937 as part of a New Deal project during the Great Depression. This tremendous technical effort entailed cutting the road into cliffs and constructing multiple bridges, including the renowned Bixby Creek Bridge, which is still one of the most photographed locations on the route.

The building of the highway revolutionized the region, opening up previously inaccessible places and bolstering local economies via increased tourism. The Pacific Coast Highway immediately became regarded as one of the world's most picturesque drives, bringing travellers from all over the world to see its breathtaking landscapes and unique attractions.

Over the years, the Pacific Coast Highway has played an important part in California's cultural and economic growth. It has become immortalized in literature, song, and cinema, representing the freedom and adventure of the open road. The Mamas & The Papas' song

"California Dreamin'" and the film "Big Sur" encapsulate the spirit of the highway and its influence on the American imagination.

The PCH has also been significant. During World War II, the roadway was strategically crucial for coastal defense, with military facilities and lookout posts located across the route. In the postwar era, the highway aided the rise of California's tourist sector, contributing to the state's image as a top travel destination.

Today, the Pacific Coast Highway is an important route for both local and tourist traffic. It continues to inspire artists, authors, and adventurers due to its natural beauty and feeling of boundless possibilities. The highway is more than simply a means of getting from point A to point B; it is a destination in and of itself, providing numerous chances for exploration and discovery.

The importance of the PCH goes beyond its visual and cultural value. It also contributes significantly to the conservation of California's coastal ecosystem. Many stretches of the route pass beside protected areas and state parks, which contribute to the preservation of the region's natural beauty and biodiversity. Efforts to preserve and enhance the highway are ongoing, with initiatives aimed at increasing safety, decreasing environmental impact, and conserving the historic integrity of this renowned route.

To summarize, the Pacific Coast Highway is more than just a route; it represents California's natural beauty, cultural diversity, and spirit of adventure. Whether you're a first-time visitor or a seasoned tourist, a trip along the PCH guarantees an amazing experience that highlights the best of what the Golden State has to offer. From the breathtaking cliffs of Big Sur to the cosmopolitan magnificence of San Francisco, the Pacific Coast Highway exemplifies the timeless fascination of the open road and the limitless possibilities it promises.

## Planning Your Trip
## (What You Should Know Before You Go)

Travelling along the Pacific Coast Highway (PCH) guarantees a quaint trip unlike any other. This historic route, which spans more than 650 miles along California's gorgeous coastline, is a magnet for tourists looking for breathtaking views, quaint coastal villages and unforgettable road trip experiences. However, just like any great adventure, a successful trip along the PCH requires careful planning and consideration of the ideal times to go.

### Understanding The Pacific Coast Highway:

Before getting into the technicalities of planning your vacation, it's critical to understand the fascination of the Pacific Coast Highway. This highway, also known as Highway 1, passes through some of California's most scenic scenery, including cliffs, golden beaches and wide ocean views. From the foggy coasts of Northern California to the sun-kissed beaches of

Southern California, every length of the PCH has its own distinct charm and natural beauty.

**Best Time to Travel:**

The appeal of the PCH changes dramatically throughout the year, thus seasonal preparation is essential for a pleasant visit.

**Spring (March to May):** Springtime on the PCH delivers blooming wildflowers, pleasant temps and fewer visitors than peak summer months. This season provides perfect circumstances for hiking coastal paths, visiting botanical gardens, and relaxing in coastal villages before the summer rush.

**Summer (June to August):** Summer is the peak tourist season along the PCH, with long days of sunlight and exciting beach activities. While the weather is usually at its finest during these months, anticipate increased traffic and higher lodging costs, particularly in famous places like Big Sur and Malibu. During this busy season, it is best to plan ahead of time and arrange your lodgings.

**Fall (September to November):** Autumn gives a welcome change to the PCH, as people thin out, temps decrease significantly and the countryside turns amber and gold. This season is perfect for whale viewing along the coast and attending local harvest festivities in coastal communities. The weather remains favourable, making it a popular choice for those wanting a calmer, more relaxed experience.

**Winter (December–February):** Winter on the PCH is marked by colder temperatures and periodic rain showers, especially in Northern California. While certain coastal activities can be limited owing to weather, winter provides unique possibilities, such as seeing migrating gray whales off the coast or spending nice nights by the fireside at seaside inns. It is important to verify road conditions, particularly in more rural places, as winter storms can occasionally disrupt travel along specific parts of the roadway.

Special Events and Festivals:

Aside from seasonal factors, organizing your journey along the PCH might coincide with particular events and festivals that enrich your experience:

- **Monterey Jazz Festival (September):** One of the world's longest-running jazz festivals, held in Monterey, draws music fans from all over the world.

*Monterey Jazz Festival*

**-Pebble Beach Concours d'Elegance (August):** A prominent automobile event displaying rare classic cars and luxury vehicles set against the picturesque background of Pebble Beach's coastline.

**-Big Sur International Marathon (April):** This scenic marathon follows the PCH route through the stunning scenery of Big Sur, attracting both runners and spectators.

# Tips For Driving on The Highway

Driving the Pacific Coast Highway (PCH) is a stunning experience, winding along the magnificent California coastline with views right out of a dream. To properly appreciate this adventure, it's important to understand and follow the laws and regulations that assure everyone's safety and happiness.

**Speed Limits:** Feel the breeze, not the rush.
The PCH is known for its beautiful splendour, but its curving roadways need caution. Speed restrictions normally range from 25 to 55 mph. In residential and frequently travelled regions, particularly in lovely coastal communities such as Malibu and Monterey, the speed limit might be reduced to 25 or 30 mph. It's essential to follow these guidelines not just to avoid fines, but also to fully appreciate the relaxed pace that allows you to take in the spectacular ocean vistas and cliffs.

**Seatbelts:** Embrace safety, embrace life. California law requires that all passengers wear seatbelts. This simple act of tightening your seatbelt is an important safety precaution, providing peace of mind while you traverse the PCH's serpentine twists. It's more than simply a rule; it's a kind gesture for your safety.

**Cell phones:** Eyes on the road, hearts in the journey. Distracted driving poses a big risk that's why California law restricts the use of portable devices while driving. This rule urges you to maintain your gaze on the road and your heart in the journey. If you need to make a phone call, use hands-free equipment but ideally, let the beauty of the PCH capture your whole attention.

**DUI:** Drive sober and enjoy the moment. Driving under the influence of alcohol or drugs is completely prohibited and punishable. The legal blood alcohol content (BAC) limit for most drivers is 0.08%, while those under 21 have a BAC of 0.01%. The PCH is a road designed to be enjoyed with clarity and presence, enabling the breathtaking scenery to make an unforgettable impression on your spirit.

**Passing and Lane Use:** Patience is the Key.
Passing lanes are not common throughout several portions of the PCH due to the road's small, twisting character. When you encounter delayed traffic, be patient and wait for authorized passing lanes. Remember that the journey down the PCH is as much about the experience as the destination. Accept the slower speed; it is part of the highway's beauty.

**Pedestrian crossings**: Respect the Stride of Life. The PCH passes through several small towns and seaside areas, with multiple pedestrian crossings. Always yield to pedestrians. These crossings are more than simply road markings; they are invitations to engage with the rich local life that punctuates your route.

**Wildlife and Scenic Areas:** Harmonize with Nature. The PCH passes through some of

California's most pristine natural areas. Signs warning of animal crossings are not difficult to find. Keep a close eye on animals, especially at dawn and dusk when they are most active. This regard for nature guarantees that your travel is peaceful and that you see the natural beauty of the shore.

**Parking**: Pause to Appreciate.
Parking along the PCH can be difficult, particularly near renowned attractions such as Big Sur and Hearst Castle. Always park in appropriate places; never obstruct the roadway or park in unlawful zones. These laws guarantee that everyone can safely halt to take in the breathtaking surroundings without creating any problems.

**Emergency vehicles:** Compassion on Wheels.
When you hear sirens or see flashing lights, pull to the side of the road and stop. California law mandates motorists to yield to emergency vehicles. This act of surrendering is a simple act

of kindness that might make a big impact on someone's life.

**Motorcycle Regulations:** Freedom and Responsibility.

The PCH is popular among motorcyclists because of its thrilling twists and panoramic vistas. Motorcyclists must wear helmets at all times and adhere to the same traffic laws as vehicles. This combination of freedom and responsibility guarantees a joyful yet safe ride.

**Cyclists:** Share the road, share the joy

Many people dream about cycling the Pacific Coast Highway. Drivers must give bicycles at least three feet of room while passing. This mutual respect and understanding makes the ride safer and more pleasurable for everyone on the road.

Driving the PCH is about more than simply getting to your destination; it's also about enjoying the ride. Following these rules and regulations ensures that your journey is safe, courteous and enjoyable. The PCH calls with its unsurpassed beauty, requiring only that you travel with caution and regard. So tighten your seatbelt, put aside your distractions and let the Pacific Coast Highway reveal its charm to you, one stunning mile at a time.

## Practical Tips for Travellers

Regardless of when you decide to drive along the PCH, here are some helpful hints to guarantee a smooth and pleasurable trip:

1. **Plan lodgings in Advance:** Securing lodgings well in advance is extremely important during peak season, particularly in famous areas such as Santa Barbara and Carmel-by-the-Sea.

2. **Check Road Conditions:** The PCH is occasionally closed and under construction, particularly following winter storms. Before leaving, check the road conditions and any advisories to prevent unexpected delays.

3. **Pack Appropriately**: Coastal weather may be unpredictable, so bring layers and basics like sunscreen and appropriate walking shoes for exploring beaches and trails.

4. **Explore Beyond the Highway**: While the PCH itself provides breathtaking vistas, don't be afraid to visit adjacent state parks, vineyards, and quaint coastal villages to immerse yourself in the region's beauty and culture fully.

Thus, planning a trip down the Pacific Coast Highway is an opportunity to discover one of California's most famous and magnificent scenery. Understanding the optimal times to visit and taking into account seasonal subtleties will allow you to optimize your trip and create lasting memories along this picturesque path. Each season along this Highway has its distinct appeal and opportunity for exploration. With careful preparation and a sense of adventure, your trip along the Pacific Coast Highway will be an amazing journey through some of America's most breathtaking coastal landscapes.

## Essential Packing List for Travelling the Pacific Coast Highway

Packing the necessary items is crucial to ensuring a smooth and pleasurable journey. Here's a detailed packing list made just for your PCH excursion, to keep you comfortable, equipped, and ready to make the most of this historic route.

### Clothing Essentials

Travelling the PCH exposes you to various microclimates, ranging from foggy northern shores to bright southern beaches. Here's everything you'll need:

**Layered Clothing:** Because the weather may be unpredictable, bring lightweight layers like T-shirts, long sleeves, and a multipurpose jacket. This allows you to effortlessly adjust to changing temperatures while remaining comfortable during your travel.

**Comfy Footwear:** Whether you're hiking through redwood woods, strolling along coastal pathways, or visiting attractive seaside villages, comfy shoes are essential. Bring durable walking shoes for outdoor excursions and casual sandals or flip-flops for beach visits. A pair of dressier shoes might come in helpful while dining at upscale establishments.

**Weather-appropriate gear:** Be prepared for any sort of weather. A lightweight rain jacket is vital for unexpected coastal drizzles, and a thick fleece will keep you warm on cold evenings. To protect yourself from the harsh California heat, carry a hat, sunglasses, and lots of sunscreen.

Travel and Safety Gear

When travelling over the PCH, safety, and navigation are critical.

**Navigation Tools**: While digital maps on your smartphone or GPS are useful, keeping a printed map of the PCH is a good backup. In some regions, mobile connectivity may be restricted, so having an accurate map might be life-saving.

**Emergency Kit:** Safety first! Bring a first-aid kit, a flashlight with additional batteries, and a multi-tool. An emergency roadside package comprising jumper cables, a tire repair kit, and reflective warning triangles is essential in case of a car breakdown.

**Reusable Water Bottle:** Hydration is essential, especially if you want to trek or spend time at the beach. A refillable water bottle keeps you hydrated while simultaneously reducing plastic waste.

### Comfort and Convenience
The key to making your journey more pleasant and pleasurable is convenience.

**Snacks and Cooler:** Keep your energy levels up with nutritious snacks such as almonds, fruit, and granola bars. A small cooler may hold beverages and other perishable foods, making it ideal for impromptu picnics at breathtaking overlooks.

**Blanket and Travel cushion:** Whether you're going on a beach picnic, stargazing, or taking a roadside nap, a soft blanket and a small travel cushion may make your stops more pleasant.

A compact backpack is perfect for day excursions and short treks. Choose one with several compartments to keep your items tidy and accessible.

## Tech Essentials

Stay connected and charged up on your trip:
**Power Bank:** Keep your gadgets charged when you don't have access to a power outlet for an extended period. A high-capacity power bank keeps your phone, camera, and other devices working.

**Chargers and cords:** Pack additional chargers and cables for your gadgets. Consider using a vehicle charger with numerous USB connections to keep everything powered while on the run.

**Portable Wi-Fi Hotspot:** In places with poor cell coverage, a portable Wi-Fi hotspot can assist you in navigating and communicating.

Entertainment and Documentary

Capture and savour each minute of your adventure.

**Camera and Accessories:** The PCH provides several picture opportunities. Bring a camera with additional batteries and memory cards to capture the breathtaking countryside, animals, and lovely villages.

**Travel diary:** Use a travel diary to record your journey. Writing down your experiences, ideas, and favourite sites not only helps to retain your memories but also adds a personal touch to your vacation.

**Entertainment:** Audiobooks, music playlists, and podcasts may make long drives more entertaining. Download them ahead of time to guarantee that you have entertainment even in locations without an internet connection.

## Health & Hygiene

To stay fresh and healthy on the go, pack travel-sized amenities including toothpaste, toothbrushes, shampoo, and conditioner. Hand sanitizer and wet wipes are useful for fast cleanups during your journey.

**Drugs**: Make sure you have any essential drugs and a copy of your prescriptions. A simple first-aid kit with bandages, disinfectant wipes, and pain medications might be beneficial for minor injuries.

**Sun Protection:** Use sunscreen, SPF lip balm, and after-sun lotion to calm your skin after a day of sun exposure.

A few more suggestions to enhance your trip are:

**Pack Smart:** Use packing cubes to arrange your belongings and make it easy to locate what you need. Rolling clothing saves space and reduces wrinkles.

**Prepare for the Unexpected**: Weather and road conditions can change rapidly. Always pack an additional pair of clothes and check the weather prediction before beginning each day.

**Leave Room for Souvenirs:** From local crafts to seashore treasures, you're bound to come across one-of-a-kind goods along the journey. Make sure you have enough room in your suitcase for these treasured memories.

Travelling the Pacific Coast Highway is an adventure packed with spectacular views, quaint villages, and different scenery. By packing intelligently, you'll be well-prepared to enjoy every moment of your travel and make memories that last a lifetime.

# CHAPTER 2

# SAN FRANCISCO: THE STARTING POINT

San Francisco, the City by the Bay, is the ideal starting place for your Pacific Coast Highway excursion. This lively metropolis combines historic history, diversified culture, and breathtaking natural beauty. From the breathtaking Golden Gate Bridge to the interesting stories of Alcatraz Island, San Francisco has a variety of renowned structures and distinct neighbourhoods that will captivate your senses and set the tone for your trip along the PCH.

## Top Attractions

**Golden Gate Bridge:** No visit to San Francisco is complete without seeing the Golden Gate Bridge, an engineering wonder that serves as the city's icon. This beautiful orange-red suspension bridge stretches 1.7 miles across the Golden Gate Strait, linking San Francisco and Marin County. Whether you walk, bike, or drive over, the sights are breathtaking.

The Golden Gate Bridge, constructed in 1937, was the world's longest and highest suspension bridge at the time. It is remarkable not just for its outstanding numbers, but also for its aesthetic appeal. The bridge's Art Deco design and vivid International Orange hue were chosen to increase visibility in the city's regular fog, resulting in a picture-perfect image against the blue Pacific.

For an amazing experience, go to the Golden Gate Bridge Welcome Center. You may learn about the bridge's history, construction, and significance through interactive exhibitions. Nearby, Crissy Field provides an excellent vantage point for photographs, with the bridge rising magnificently above the water, frequently shrouded in a magical veil of fog.

**Alcatraz Island:**

Alcatraz Island, which houses the iconic old federal penitentiary, is only a short boat ride from the city's shore. Alcatraz, also known as **"The Rock,"** housed some of America's most notorious criminals, including Al Capone and Robert Stroud, the "Birdman of Alcatraz." The island's isolation in the middle of San Francisco

Bay made it an ideal location for a maximum-security prison, and it's surrounded by chilling stories of daring escape attempts and life inside its imposing walls.

A visit to Alcatraz provides an immersive experience that transports you back in time. The audio tour, conducted by former convicts and guards, provides a detailed depiction of daily life on the island. You'll hear firsthand descriptions of escape attempts, prison riots, and the boredom of solitary confinement.

Aside from its jail past, Alcatraz Island has lovely gardens, tide pools, and bird colonies, making it an intriguing trip for wildlife enthusiasts as well. The contrast between its tragic past and its peaceful present is startling, allowing a better understanding of this unique monument.

Best Neighbourhoods

**Fisherman's Wharf:**

Fisherman's Wharf is a vibrant waterfront district that embodies San Francisco's nautical past. It's a must-see for anybody visiting the city, thanks to its bustling ambiance, great seafood, and family-friendly activities.

Begin your tour at Pier 39, where sea lions relax in the sun and delight visitors with their lively antics. The pier is crowded with stores, restaurants, and attractions, including the Aquarium of the Bay, which allows visitors to stroll through tunnels surrounded by aquatic life from San Francisco Bay.

For a sample of the city's gastronomic specialties, visit one of the numerous seafood stalls and restaurants that surround the waterfront. Local specialties include fresh

Dungeness crab, clam chowder served in sourdough bread bowls, and fish and chips.

Fisherman's Wharf also houses ancient ships in the Maritime National Historical Park, where visitors can board boats such as the Balclutha, a 19th-century square rigger, and the Eureka, a paddlewheel ferry. Each ship offers a tale about the city's maritime history, providing insight into the life of the sailors who once called these vessels home.

**Chinatown:**

San Francisco's Chinatown is the oldest and one of the largest in North America. Stepping through the majestic Dragon Gate at Grant Avenue and Bush Street takes you into a colourful world of busy shops, exotic fragrances, and rich cultural history.

Chinatown provides a sensory feast. The sidewalks are crowded with stores that offer everything from traditional Chinese medicines and teas to vibrant silk clothes and beautiful jade jewelry. Foodies will enjoy a variety of traditional Chinese cuisine, from dim sum at well-known eateries like Yank Sing to sweet delicacies at the Golden Gate Fortune Cookie Factory, where you can see fortune cookies being created by hand.

Chinatown has several cultural landmarks. The Tin How Temple, devoted to the Chinese sea goddess Mazu, provides a peaceful respite from the busy streets below. The Chinese Historical Society of America Museum sheds light on Chinese immigrants' contributions to the city and the obstacles they encountered.

Chinatown is more than a neighbourhood, it is a live, breathing community that has preserved its customs and culture despite the city's ever-changing terrain. It's a site where history and the present combine, providing tourists with an unforgettable and fascinating experience.

**Mission District:**

The Mission District, also known as "The Mission," is the cultural hub of San Francisco's Latino community. This bustling area is noted for its bright murals, varied mix of shops and eateries, and exciting street festivals.

Mission Dolores is San Francisco's oldest surviving edifice and is located in the heart of the Mission District. This historic mission, founded in 1776, commemorates the city's early Spanish colonial past. The neighbouring Mission Dolores Park is a popular meeting location for both locals and visitors, with breathtaking views of the city skyline.

The streets of the Mission District serve as an outdoor mural art exhibition. The Precita Eyes Mural Arts Center provides guided tours of the neighbourhood's most prominent murals, each portraying a tale of community, suffering, and survival. Balmy Alley and Clarion Alley are well-known for their vivid and thought-provoking artworks.

Food is a vital component of the Mission District experience. The area is home to some of the city's top taquerias, such as La Taqueria and El Farolito, where you can eat delicious tacos and burros. For a taste of modern food, visit one of the many trendy eateries and cafés that have popped up alongside classic Mexican establishments.

The Mission District is a vibrant fusion of old and new, where cultural history and contemporary innovation meet. It's a community that encourages exploration and rewards those who take the time to uncover its various facets.

San Francisco, with its renowned monuments and numerous neighbourhoods, provides the backdrop for an amazing ride down the Pacific Coast Highway. From the beautiful Golden Gate Bridge to the ancient streets of Chinatown and the vibrant culture of the Mission District, the city provides a diverse range of experiences that will leave an indelible impact. Let San Francisco's sights, sounds, and tales inspire and lead you on your PCH excursion.

## Dining and Accommodation Recommendations

**Dining in San Francisco:**

San Francisco is also known for its culinary diversity, and has a wide range of eating options to suit every taste. Whether you're a gourmet, a fan of street cuisine or looking for a genuine cultural experience, the city's eating scene is sure to be a highlight of your trip.

**Gary Danko** in Fisherman's Wharf is a great option for people searching for a premium dining experience. Gary Danko, known for its superb service and classy environment, serves a seasonal cuisine that includes delicious delicacies like roasted lobster, herb-crusted lamb, and a variety of artisanal cheeses. Each dish exemplifies the restaurant's commitment to quality and taste, providing an outstanding culinary experience.

Another hidden treasure is **Quince**, which is located in the Financial District. This three-Michelin-starred restaurant is located in a historic structure and has an air of elegance and refinement. Quince's menu varies daily to reflect the freshest products from local farmers. Signature delicacies such as white truffle risotto and dry-aged duck breast are complemented with a wide wine selection carefully picked to complement your dining experience.

**Casual Dining and Cafés:** Tartine Bakery in the Mission District offers a more casual yet equally delicious dining experience. Tartine, known for its freshly made bread, pastries, and sandwiches, is a foodie's dream. Enjoy a warm croissant or a substantial slice of their country bread while enjoying a freshly prepared cup of coffee.

If you're craving seafood, **Swan Oyster Depot** is a must-stop. This no-frills diner on Polk Street has been offering fresh fish since 1912. Order a plate of oysters, clam chowder or the famous crab Louie salad and enjoy the taste of the ocean in a bustling, colourful atmosphere.

**Ethnic cuisine:** San Francisco's rich cultural tapestry is mirrored in its diversified ethnic eating scene. Z & Y Restaurant in Chinatown serves traditional Sichuan food, including spicy cumin lamb and Dan Dan noodles, which are sure to tickle your taste buds. The bright atmosphere and historic decor enhance the whole eating experience.

Tony's Pizza Napoletana in North Beach is the best place to get a taste of Italy. Tony's, known for its award-winning pizzas, serves a range of varieties, including classic Neapolitan, New York, and Sicilian. The Margherita pizza, which is crafted with San Marzano tomatoes and fresh mozzarella, is a fan favourite.

## Accommodation in San Francisco

Finding the ideal hotel to stay in San Francisco is an essential component of your vacation experience. Whether you like luxurious hotels, lovely boutique inns or affordable hostels, the city has something for everyone.

**Luxury Hotels:**

For those seeking elegance, the Ritz-Carlton in Nob Hill offers an excellent getaway. This five-star hotel offers large rooms with breathtaking city views, stylish design and first-rate services. The Ritz-Carlton's spa and fine dining restaurant, Parallel 37, add to the luxury experience.

Another excellent choice is the **Fairmont San Francisco.** Perched atop Nob Hill, this historic hotel provides exquisite suites with a mix of traditional elegance and modern comfort. The Fairmont's spectacular rooftop garden and the

Tonga Room & Hurricane Lounge, a distinctive tiki-themed lounge, are must-sees.

Boutique hotels:

**Hotel Drisco** in Pacific Heights offers a more intimate and customized experience. This boutique hotel, set in a lovely Edwardian structure, has nicely decorated rooms, a complimentary breakfast, and evening wine receptions. The peaceful surroundings and dedicated service make Hotel Drisco an excellent choice for discriminating guests.

**The Inn at Union Square** located in the center of the city, offers a comfortable and convenient stay. With its attractive design, daily continental breakfast and evening wine and cheese receptions, this boutique hotel creates a warm and welcoming environment that seems like a home away from home.

Budget-Friendly Alternatives:

**HI San Francisco Downtown Hostel** is a go-to here, as it offers pleasant rooms for budget-conscious travellers. This hostel, located near Union Square, provides both dormitory and private rooms. With its bright common spaces, planned events, and friendly staff, the HI San Francisco Downtown Hostel is a fantastic starting point for experiencing the city.

**The Green Tortoise Hostel** in North Beach is another budget-friendly choice. The Green Tortoise, known for its vibrant social scene and complimentary meals, provides a stimulating and interesting stay for budget-conscious guests. The hostel's closeness to sights such as Coit Tower and Fisherman's Wharf enhances its attractiveness.

### Day Trips & Nearby Attractions In San Francisco

San Francisco's outstanding location gives it an excellent starting point for visiting a range of local sites. From natural wonders to quaint villages, there are plenty of intriguing day excursions to make your vacation more memorable.

**Muir Woods National Monument:**
Muir Woods National Monument located a short drive north of the city, provides a peaceful getaway into nature. This park, known for its towering old-growth redwood trees, offers a tranquil atmosphere for hiking and photography. The main track is a stroll ideal for all ages, while more daring hikers may explore the neighbouring trails for a more demanding experience. The magnificence of the redwoods, some of which are over 600 years old, is incredibly breathtaking and provides a dramatic contrast to San Francisco's metropolitan backdrop.

**Sausalito:**
Sausalito, just across the Golden Gate Bridge, is a lovely village. Sausalito, with its picturesque waterfront, art galleries and boutique stores, is an ideal place for a relaxing day trip. Stroll down the picturesque promenade, have a seafood lunch

at one of the waterfront restaurants, and visit the local stores and galleries. Take a boat journey back to San Francisco and enjoy breathtaking views of the city skyline and the water.

**Napa Valley:**
Wine fans will find nirvana in Napa Valley, which is roughly an hour's drive from San Francisco. Napa Valley, known for its world-class wines and stunning vineyards, provides a day of indulgence and leisure. Visit notable vineyards like Robert Mondavi and Domaine Carneros, take a picturesque drive down the Silverado Trail, and dine at one of the valley's renowned restaurants. Napa Valley is a wonderful day trip because of its superb wine, exquisite gastronomy, and magnificent landscape.

**Half-Moon Bay:**
Half Moon Bay, located south of San Francisco, provides a magnificent seaside escape. This location is ideal for outdoor enthusiasts since it boasts cliffs, sandy beaches, and green farmland.

Explore the tidal pools at Fitzgerald Marine Reserve, go for a lovely trek along the coastal cliffs, or rest on the sandy sands at Half Moon Bay State Beach. The quaint downtown area, with its local shops and restaurants, adds to the allure of this seaside jewel.

**Point Reyes National Seashore:**
Point Reyes National Seashore is a great place to spend the day admiring nature and wildlife. This protected region, located approximately an hour and a half from San Francisco, is home to stunning coastal cliffs, large beaches, and a rich environment. Hike to the historic Point Reyes Lighthouse, observe migrating whales from the cliffs, or explore the wildflower-filled meadows in the spring. The opportunity to observe tule elk, harbour seals, and a variety of bird species adds to the appeal of this unspoiled coastal retreat.

**Santa Cruz:**
Santa Cruz, located farther down the coast, is a thriving beach town that combines natural

beauty with energetic activities. Spend the day at the Santa Cruz Beach Boardwalk, one of the country's oldest amusement parks, or stroll around downtown's distinctive shops and eateries. Nature enthusiasts may take a trek in the adjacent Henry Cowell Redwoods State Park or travel along Highway 1 for breathtaking coastal vistas.

**Monterey and Carmel by- the-Sea:**
Monterey and Carmel-by-the-Sea are a bit further away, but worth the drive. Visit the famed Monterey Bay Aquarium, walk down Cannery Row, and experience the historic Fisherman's Wharf. Carmel-by-the-Sea, just south of Monterey, is a lovely community with an eclectic mix of art galleries, boutique stores and excellent dining options. The gorgeous 17-mile Drive, with its spectacular coastline vistas and renowned monuments such as the Lone Cypress, is a must-see during your tour.

Each of these days excursions and neighbouring sites offer a distinct experience that will enhance your vacation to San Francisco. Whether you're looking for natural beauty, cultural enrichment, or gastronomic pleasures, the surrounding locations provide several options for adventure and exploration.

# CHAPTER 3

## SAN FRANCISCO TO SANTA CRUZ

The Pacific Coast Highway, which runs from San Francisco to Santa Cruz, provides a beautiful excursion packed with stunning coastal landscapes, attractive communities, and a variety of tranquil and exciting adventures. This section of Highway 1 is well-known for its stunning cliffs, rolling waves and infinite horizon, making it a must-see for any visitor looking for the ultimate California road trip.

### Pacifica (The Coastal Gem):

Leaving the frenetic bustle of San Francisco behind, your first destination will be the beach village of Pacifica. Pacifica, located between the Santa Cruz Mountains and the Pacific Ocean, provides a peaceful vacation with its scenic splendour and laid-back atmosphere. The town's beaches are less congested than those in the metropolis, making them ideal for relaxing and admiring nature.

**Mori Point:**

Mori Point, located inside the Golden Gate National Recreation Area, is a hidden gem in Pacifica. This picturesque cliff provides sweeping views of the Pacific Ocean and rough shoreline. Hikers can explore a range of paths, ranging from short treks to more difficult routes, all with breathtaking views. On a clear day, you could see migratory whales in the distance. The wildflowers here, especially in the spring, provide a pop of colour to an already beautiful scene.

**Pacifica State Beach (Linda Mar Beach):**

Another must-see destination is Pacifica State Beach, better known as Linda Mar Beach. This crescent-shaped beach is renowned among surfers due to its regular waves. If you are new to surfing, numerous local schools provide training to assist you catch your first wave. For those who prefer to stay on land, the beach is ideal for taking a stroll, making sandcastles or having a picnic with a view.

**Half Moon Bay (A Serene Retreat):**

Continuing south, you'll reach Half Moon Bay, a tiny town famed for its attractive centre, verdant countryside and stunning beaches. Half Moon Bay's beachfront atmosphere offers a peaceful escape, making it an ideal stop on your journey.

**Pillar Point Harbor:**

Pillar Point Harbor is a busy harbour where you can see fishermen unload their daily catch. It's an excellent spot to eat fresh seafood at one of the harborside restaurants or purchase some to cook later. If you travel during the winter, keep an eye out for the legendary Mavericks surf break, where courageous surfers take on some of the world's largest waves.

**Half Moon Bay State Beach:**

Half Moon Bay State Beach runs for kilometers and provides adequate room for beachcombing, sunbathing, and birding. The Coastal Trail follows the shore, providing a lovely route for walking, running, or cycling. The sound of breaking waves and the view of the infinite ocean make this an ideal place to relax.

**Downtown Half Moon Bay:**

Downtown Half Moon Bay is charming, with Victorian-style buildings, unusual shops, and quiet cafés. Wander around the streets, seeing art galleries and boutiques, and maybe stopping for a coffee or lunch at one of the local restaurants. The town is also known for its annual Pumpkin Festival, which draws tourists from all around with its massive pumpkins, colourful procession, and family-friendly activities.

## Exploring Santa Cruz: Boardwalk & Surfing Spots

As you leave Half Moon Bay, the scenery begins to change, indicating your approach to Santa Cruz. This thriving coastal town is recognized for its diverse culture, breathtaking coastline, and outdoor sports. Whether you choose action or relaxation, Santa Cruz offers something for everyone.

**The Santa Cruz Beach Boardwalk:**

A vacation to Santa Cruz isn't complete without a trip to the Santa Cruz Beach Boardwalk. This iconic coastal amusement park evokes a bygone age, replete with roller coasters, carnival games, and cotton candy. The historic Giant Dipper roller coaster, inaugurated in 1924, provides a thrilling ride with stunning views of the ocean. For a more leisurely experience, ride the Looff Carousel, which goes back to 1911. The boardwalk also features a range of restaurants, ranging from typical boardwalk food to more modern eating alternatives.

**West Cliff Drive:**

A picturesque drive or bike ride along West Cliff Drive provides a panoramic view of Santa Cruz's coastline. This lovely route follows the coastline, providing breathtaking views of the ocean as well as access to various great beaches and surf locations. Along the way, you'll pass by the Santa Cruz Surfing Museum, which is housed in a historic lighthouse and documents the history of surfing in Santa Cruz and beyond.

**Surfing Spots:**

Santa Cruz is known as the surf capital of Northern California, and it's simple to understand why. It's a mecca for surfers of all skill levels, thanks to its steady waves and diverse breaks.

**Steamers Lane:**

Steamer Lane is one of Santa Cruz's most recognized surf areas. Steamer Lane, known for its huge waves and tough conditions, draws expert surfers from all over the world. Even if you're not a surfer, it's worth going only to see the pros surf from the safety of the cliffs above.

**Cowell's Beach:**

Cowell's Beach is an ideal area for novices to learn how to surf. The waves here are gentler, making them excellent for beginners. Several surf schools operate in the vicinity, providing training and equipment rental. The beach is also an excellent area to unwind and enjoy the sun.

**Pleasure Point:**

Pleasure Point is another renowned surfing area with a range of breakers to suit all ability levels. The region offers a relaxed atmosphere, with both residents and visitors enjoying the surf.

After your surf lesson, stop by one of the surrounding cafés or food trucks for a bite to eat.

**Natural Bridges State Beach:**

Aside from surfing, Santa Cruz has many other natural attractions. Natural Bridges State Beach is renowned for its unique rock formations and tidal pools. It's also an excellent site to go bird watching, and in the winter, you may view monarch butterflies migrating through the region.

**Santa Cruz Wharf:**

For a more urban atmosphere, go to Santa Cruz Wharf. This lengthy pier runs into Monterey Bay and houses restaurants, stores, and fishing sites. It's a terrific area to take a stroll, eat fresh seafood, and even see sea lions lazing on the pilings below.

**Downtown Santa Cruz:**

Downtown Santa Cruz is a busy neighbourhood with a variety of stores, restaurants, and entertainment options. Stroll along Pacific Avenue, where you'll discover a mix of independent boutiques, vintage shops, and big chain businesses. The region also holds several events throughout the year, such as farmers markets, street festivals, and live music performances.

Conclusion, the journey from San Francisco to Santa Cruz along the Pacific Coast Highway is more than simply a drive; it's an experience of some of California's most gorgeous and diverse scenery. From the tranquil beaches of Pacifica and Half Moon Bay to Santa Cruz's bustling culture and outdoor adventures, this itinerary is jam-packed with unforgettable experiences and magnificent scenery. Whether you're a surfer, a hiker, or just someone who enjoys exploring, this section of the Pacific Coast Highway guarantees a memorable adventure.

## Natural Wonders

### Big Basin Redwoods State Park:

While Santa Cruz's shoreline and surf culture may pique your interest, a visit to Big Basin Redwoods State Park provides a different type of natural beauty. Big Basin, California's first state park, is located just a short drive from Santa Cruz. It was created in 1902. It is home to ancient coast redwoods, some of which are more than 2,500 years old and stand over 300 feet tall.

This Park covers 18,000 acres and has a range of routes suitable for hikers of all skill levels. The Redwood Loop Trail is the park's main attraction, a 0.6-mile walk that takes you past some of the park's most spectacular trees, including the "**Father of the Forest**" and the "**Mother of the Forest.**" These giants give a humble perspective on nature's majesty.

For more daring hikers, the Berry Creek Falls Trail is a necessity. This 10.5-mile circle will take you through dense redwood woods and past four breathtaking waterfalls, including the 65-foot Berry Creek Falls. The walk might be difficult, with steep portions and uneven terrain, but the view of the waterfall pouring through the forest is well worth the effort.

**Camping and picnicking:**

Big Basin has various campsites where visitors can completely immerse themselves in the park's natural splendour. From tent camping to rustic cottages, there are accommodations to suit every taste. For those who do not wish to remain overnight, the park's picnic spots offer an ideal setting for a noon lunch under the tall trees. Remember to remove any rubbish and respect the park's natural ecosystem.

**Wildlife and Flora:**

The park is a home to not just old redwoods, but also a wide variety of species. Look out for black-tailed deer, raccoons and many bird species. The park's streams and creeks provide habitat for endangered marbled murrelets and vulnerable steelhead trout. In the spring and summer, wildflowers litter the forest floor, providing bright pops of colour to the vegetation.

## Dining and Accomodation in Santa Cruz

Santa Cruz is a gastronomic and traveller's paradise, with a varied choice of dining and lodging alternatives to suit all interests and budgets. Here's a list of the greatest places to eat and stay while in town.

### Dining in Santa Cruz

**The picnic basket:**

The Picnic Basket is a popular neighbourhood spot for a relaxed but wonderful supper. This beachside restaurant specializes in fresh, locally sourced food. Their sandwiches, salads, and desserts are ideal for a beach picnic or a fast meal after a day of touring.

**Laili Restaurant:**

For a more sophisticated experience, Laili Restaurant serves a unique combination of Mediterranean and Afghan cuisine. The outdoor courtyard is an ideal backdrop for supper, and the menu includes lamb kebabs, saffron chicken, and vegetarian alternatives.

**Stagnaro Brothers. Seafood:**

If you're in the mood for seafood, go to Stagnaro Bros. Seafood at the Santa Cruz Wharf. This family-owned restaurant has been dishing up fresh fish since 1937. Enjoy clam chowder, crab cakes, or their famed fish & chips while admiring the views of the water.

**Pizza My heart:**

For a taste of local flavour, stop by Pizza My Heart. This popular Santa Cruz pizza is famed for its large slices and surf-themed décor. It's an excellent choice for a quick, relaxed supper.

## Accomodation in Santa Cruz

**Dream Inn:**

For those wishing to stay directly on the beach, the Dream Inn has beachfront accommodations with breathtaking views. The hotel's retro-chic decor celebrates Santa Cruz's surf culture, and facilities include a heated pool, hot tub, and beachside dining.

**Chaminade Resort and Spa:**

Chaminade Resort & Spa, set in the hills above Santa Cruz, offers a more isolated and luxury experience. This historic resort features large accommodations, a full-service spa, and superb cuisine. The property's expansive grounds contain hiking paths and tennis courts, making it a peaceful escape from the hustle and bustle of town.

## Hotel Paradox

Hotel Paradox is located downtown and mixes modern design with natural elements to create a distinctive and attractive ambiance. The hotel has an outdoor pool, a fitness facility, and an on-site restaurant called Solaire that serves farm-to-table food.

## Inn at Depot Hill

For a more private and romantic encounter, the Inn at Depot Hill provides luxurious bed-and-breakfast accommodations in a historic structure. Each room is differently designed, and the inn is well-known for its excellent service and exquisite breakfasts.

## Budget Options

Santa Cruz also has a range of motels and budget-friendly hotels. The Ocean Pacific Lodge and Best Western Plus All Suites Inn offer nice lodging at a reasonable price, with convenient access to the beach and downtown.

The Pacific Coast Highway from San Francisco to Santa Cruz is a natural wonderland, complete with attractive villages and interesting activities. This route promises an amazing road trip, from the tranquil beaches of Pacifica and Half Moon Bay to Santa Cruz's bustling culture and recreational experiences, as well as the ancient magnificence of Big Basin Redwoods State Park. Whether you're relishing a gourmet dinner, catching a wave, or gazing in wonder at towering redwoods, every minute of your adventure is unique and enlightening. So, pack your bags, hit the road, and let the Pacific Coast Highway guide you through one of California's most enchanting regions.

# CHAPTER 4

# SANTA CRUZ TO MONTEREY

Travelling from Santa Cruz to Monterey on the Pacific Coast Highway (PCH) is like entering a magnificent painting. This part of Highway 1 combines a rocky coastline, pleasant communities, and historic sites, giving it the typical California experience. As you leave the colourful, beach-town feel of Santa Cruz behind, the road opens out to offer some of the most stunning scenery and interesting stops along the coast.

## Scenic Stops: Davenport and Pigeon Point Lighthouse

**Davenport:**

Davenport is a beautiful village located only a short drive south of Santa Cruz. Nestled between the majestic cliffs and the roaring Pacific Ocean, this small village of just 400 people provides a peaceful refuge from the rush and bustle of larger towns. Davenport has a long history in the whaling and timber industries, but it is currently more recognized for its natural beauty and creative culture.

Begin your trip at Davenport Beach, where the rough coastline meets exquisite sands. With its stunning sea stacks and secret caverns, this beach is a photographers' and nature lovers' dream come true. The neighbouring Davenport Bluffs provide a higher elevated viewing point, ideal for capturing panoramic vistas of the shoreline. The cliffs are an excellent place for whale watching, particularly during migration seasons.

Visit the Davenport Jail, a modest, two-cell facility erected in 1914 that is now used as a quirky museum displaying local history. Across the street, you'll discover the Davenport Roadhouse Restaurant & Inn, which is ideal for a substantial lunch or a glass of local wine. The restaurant's menu focuses on farm-to-table food, using locally produced products to accentuate the tastes of the region.

**Pigeon Point Lighthouse:**

Continuing south, you'll come with the magnificent Pigeon Point Lighthouse. Standing at 115 feet, it is one of the West Coast's highest lighthouses and has been directing seafarers since 1872. Perched on a rock, the lighthouse provides breathtaking views of the Pacific Ocean and serves as a reminder of the area's maritime past.

The Pigeon Point Light Station is not just a historical site, but also a functional hostel. The grounds are available to the public, and visitors can examine the lighthouse's base and adjacent structures. The hostel provides a unique overnight experience with breathtaking ocean views. The lighthouse's Fresnel lens, currently housed in an adjacent building, is a feat of engineering and a must-see for anyone interested in historical technology.

The surrounding region is abundant in animals. Seals and sea lions are frequently seen lounging on the rocks below, and the seas are alive with migrating grey whales at certain times of the year. The tidal pools surrounding the lighthouse are filled with marine life and provide an intriguing insight into the undersea world. There are guided tours available that provide detailed information about the lighthouse's history and the surrounding natural surroundings.

## Exploring Monterey: Cannery Row and Monterey Bay Aquarium.

**Cannery Row:** When you arrive in Monterey, the city's attractiveness and historical significance are instantly obvious. Many tourists' first destination is Cannery Row, which was popularized by John Steinbeck in his novel of the same name. Cannery Row, formerly the center of the sardine-packing business, has evolved into a lively waterfront boulevard lined with shops, restaurants, and historical landmarks.

Walking along Cannery Row, you can almost hear the echoes of the canning plants that formerly dotted the area. Much of the area's original architecture has survived, and markers along the road tell the story of the people and companies that prospered here. Cannery Row is now a busy zone where you may eat fresh seafood at one of the numerous restaurants, shop at one-of-a-kind boutiques, or simply relax on a riverside bench and enjoy the ocean views.

Don't miss Steinbeck Plaza, where you may learn more about the renowned author's life and work. Nearby, the Pacific Biological Laboratories, which was once the workplace of Steinbeck's friend Ed Ricketts, provides insight into the scientific research that inspired much of Steinbeck's writing. The building is not always open to the public, but guided tours are available on specific dates.

**Monterey Bay Aquarium** is another world-renowned marine haven. No trip to Monterey is complete without visiting the Monterey Bay Aquarium. Located at the end of Cannery Row, this world-famous facility provides an immersive experience of the marine life of the California coast. The aquarium is renowned for its commitment to marine research, conservation, and education, and it offers an unforgettable experience for visitors of all ages.

The Open marine exhibit, one of the aquarium's largest, boasts a 90-foot glass into the ocean and displays a broad assortment of marine species, including sparkling swarms of sardines, stately sea turtles, and sleek hammerhead sharks. Many people enjoy the hypnotic show of jellyfish, with their ethereal motions and vivid hues.

The Kelp Forest display is another must-see. This towering, three-story structure depicts the coastal kelp forests found just offshore and is home to a variety of fish, invertebrates, and marine species. Watching the swaying kelp and the diverse marine life that lives on it is both relaxing and educational.

The Touch Pools offer a hands-on experience with sea stars, sea urchins, and other tide pool creatures. The aquarium's knowledgeable staff and volunteers are always available to provide information and answer questions, making the visit both enjoyable and informative.

The Monterey Bay Aquarium is also at the forefront of marine conservation initiatives. The aquarium's Seafood Watch program advises visitors on sustainable seafood options, thereby helping to protect marine ecosystems for future generations. Every exhibit demonstrates the institution's commitment to conservation, making it more than just a place of wonder but also a beacon of hope for our oceans' future.

## The Road Ahead

As you leave Monterey and continue your journey along the Pacific Coast Highway, the memories of the scenic stops and experiences along the way will undoubtedly linger. From the quaint charm of Davenport and the historical beacon of Pigeon Point Lighthouse to the literary and marine wonders of Monterey, this stretch of the PCH offers a rich tapestry of experiences. Whether you're a history buff, a nature enthusiast, or simply someone seeking the beauty and tranquility of the California coast, the journey from Santa Cruz to Monterey promises to be an unforgettable adventure.

The road ahead promises even more breathtaking views and intriguing destinations, each with its own distinct story to tell. So buckle up, roll down the windows and let the Pacific breeze guide you on your next adventure.

**17-Mile Drive: Pebble Beach and scenic vistas**

After immersing yourself in the cultural and marine wonders of Monterey, the next leg of your journey takes you along the famous 17-mile Drive. This scenic route winds through the gated community of Pebble Beach, offering some of the most spectacular coastal views in California. As you enter the drive, you'll be greeted by an array of scenic pullouts, each providing a unique perspective of the rugged coastline, pristine beaches and lush forested areas.

**Pebble Beach (A Golfer's Paradise):**
Pebble Beach is synonymous with world-class golf, and its famed Pebble Beach Golf Links is a bucket-list destination for golf enthusiasts. Even

if you're not a golfer, the beauty of the meticulously maintained greens set against the backdrop of the Pacific Ocean is worth experiencing. The course has hosted numerous prestigious tournaments, including the U.S. Open, and walking its grounds offers a glimpse into golfing history.

A visit to the Lodge at Pebble Beach is a must. This luxurious resort is steeped in history and offers stunning views of the 18th hole. Even if you're not staying at the lodge, you can enjoy a meal at one of its excellent restaurants or simply relax with a drink on the terrace, taking in the panoramic ocean views. The lodge also houses a selection of upscale shops where you can find everything from golf apparel to fine jewelry.

**Scenic Vistas: Nature's Masterpieces**

As you continue along 17-Mile Drive, you'll encounter a series of scenic vistas that highlight the natural beauty of the area. Don't miss the Lone Cypress, one of the most photographed trees in North America. This iconic Monterey cypress, perched on a granite outcropping, has stood sentinel over the Pacific Ocean for more than 250 years. It's a symbol of resilience and beauty, and its dramatic setting makes for an unforgettable sight.

Another notable stop is **Bird Rock**, where you can observe a diverse array of seabirds and marine mammals. Harbour seals and sea lions often lounge on the rock, providing ample photo opportunities. The incessant chorus of seabird songs and the thundering waves create a symphony of nature that is both relaxing and exciting.

**The Ghost Tree**, another striking landmark, is named for its gnarled, bleached branches that resemble a ghostly figure. This tree, situated near Pescadero Point, stands in stark contrast to the vibrant greenery and is a favourite subject for photographers, especially at sunset when the light casts an eerie glow.

This route also takes you through Del Monte Forest, where towering Monterey pines and cypresses create a serene, woodland atmosphere. The forest is home to a variety of wildlife, and if you're lucky, you might spot deer grazing among the trees or hawks soaring overhead.

## Dining and Accommodation in Monterey

After a day of exploring the scenic wonders of 17-Mile Drive, returning to Monterey for a relaxing evening is the perfect way to cap off your adventures. Monterey offers a diverse array of dining and accommodation options to suit all tastes and budgets, ensuring a comfortable and enjoyable stay.

**Dining:**
Monterey's eating scene is a reflection of its unique cultural tapestry and seaside riches. Seafood enthusiasts will be in ecstasy here, with several eateries providing fresh catches from Monterey Bay. One of the popular eating places is The Sardine Factory, a historic restaurant that

has been serving wonderful fish meals since 1968. Located on Cannery Row, the restaurant promises an exquisite, old-world environment and a menu comprising everything from abalone bisque to lobster thermidor.

For a more informal eating experience, travel to Fisherman's Wharf, where you'll find a variety of cafes serving clam chowder, fish & chips, and other seafood classics. Old Fisherman's Grotto is a local institution famed for its award-winning clam chowder and picturesque harbour vistas.

If you're in the mood for Italian food, consider dining at **Cafe Moulin**, a charming cafe on Cannery Row providing a menu of French-inspired meals and an extensive wine list. The restaurant's small environment and tasty cuisine make it popular among residents and visitors alike.

For a sample of local farm-to-table cuisine, visit **Montrio Bistro**. Located in a historic firehouse in downtown Monterey, this restaurant emphasizes fresh cuisine obtained from local farms. The menu provides a range of inventive meals, from wood-fired pizzas to delectable steaks, all made with an emphasis on sustainability and freshness.

**Accommodation:**

Monterey provides a selection of lodgings, from lovely bed-and-breakfasts to opulent resorts, guaranteeing that you find the appropriate spot to relax after a day of discovery.

For a sumptuous stay, try renting a room at the **InterContinental The Clement Monterey.** Located on Cannery Row, this elegant hotel provides spectacular ocean views, contemporary facilities, and a convenient position close to major attractions including the Monterey Bay Aquarium. The hotel's elegant rooms and excellent service make it a popular choice among discerning travellers.

Another excellent option is the **Monterey Plaza Hotel & Spa,** which is located directly on the waterfront. This hotel combines classic elegance and modern comfort, with spacious rooms, a full-service spa, and breathtaking views of the bay. The rooftop terrace is the ideal place to relax with a cocktail while watching the sunset over the Pacific.

If you prefer a more intimate setting, the Old Monterey Inn offers a charming bed and breakfast experience. This historic property, surrounded by lush gardens, provides well-appointed rooms and personalized service. The inn's cozy atmosphere and gourmet breakfasts make it an ideal romantic getaway.

For those looking for environmentally friendly lodging, the Asilomar Conference Grounds in nearby Pacific Grove is an excellent option. This historic property, designed by renowned architect Julia Morgan, provides rustic charm and a tranquil setting just a short walk from the beach. The grounds include several lodges and cottages, offering a variety of accommodation options.

Now, you have travelled from Santa Cruz to Monterey along the Pacific Coast Highway, passing through some of California's most scenic and culturally rich destinations. From the artistic enclave of Davenport and the historic Pigeon Point Lighthouse to the literary charm of Cannery Row and the marine wonders of the Monterey Bay Aquarium, this stretch of the PCH offers a plethora of experiences.

This amazing 17-mile Drive, with its iconic landmarks and breathtaking views, is the ideal combination of natural beauty and human ingenuity. Whether you're exploring Pebble Beach's golf courses, marvelling at the Lone Cypress, or savouring fresh seafood in Monterey, this journey will provide you with memories to last a lifetime.

As you continue your adventure along the Pacific Coast Highway, each new chapter will bring its unique discoveries and delights. So, keep your camera ready, your curiosity engaged, and your sense of wonder alive as you drive this legendary route. The Pacific Coast Highway is not just a route; it's a journey through the heart and soul of California's coastal beauty.

# CHAPTER 5

## MONTEREY TO BIG SUR

Nestled along the rocky California coast, the route from Monterey to Big Sur is a magnificent symphony that captivates the senses and transports visitors to a realm of natural splendour. This part of the Pacific Coast Highway (Highway 1) has its beautiful scenery, iconic monuments and thrilling combination of sea and sky. As you begin on your adventure, expect to be captivated by the grandeur of Bixby Creek Bridge and the ethereal beauty of McWay Falls.

**Bixby Creek Bridge**

Bixby Creek Bridge, built in 1932, is one of the most photographed structures on the West Coast. As you approach the bridge, you can see its magnificent arch and thin piers, which span 714 feet over a steep canyon cut by Bixby Creek. The contrast between this man-made masterpiece and the raw beauty of Big Sur is breathtaking.

Standing at the bridge's edge, the Pacific Ocean spreads out before you, its waves breaking against the rocks far below. The bridge, a testimony to early twentieth-century engineering, blends effortlessly into the natural terrain. The vista is especially beautiful around sunset when the sky is painted in orange, pink, and purple, spreading a golden light over the whole region.

Bixby Creek Bridge provides a limitless number of options for photographers and nature lovers to get the ideal snap. Whether you're shooting photographs from one of the numerous overlooks or just admiring the scenery, the bridge represents the ongoing fascination of the Big Sur coastline.

**McWay Falls**

Continuing south along Highway 1, the route travels through deep woods and along sheer cliffs, affording enticing vistas of the ocean at every bend. Julia Pfeiffer Burns State Park, located about 12 miles south of Bixby Creek Bridge, is home to McWay Falls, one of Big Sur's most renowned natural beauties.

McWay Falls is an 80-foot waterfall that cascades directly onto a pristine beach, a rare and breathtaking sight that few places in the world can match. The sight of the waterfalls cascading smoothly into the turquoise waters of a remote cove is nothing short of magnificent. The surrounding cliffs and lush vegetation create a peaceful, almost otherworldly atmosphere.

To truly admire McWay Falls, follow the short trek from the parking area to the viewpoint. As you go down the walkway, the waterfall becomes louder, merging with the distant roar of the ocean waves. The view from the overlook is awe-inspiring, affording a fantastic vantage point to gaze at the falls and the cove below.

McWay Falls represents the raw, unspoiled beauty that defines Big Sur. It's a place where you can lose yourself in nature's tranquility and form a deep connection with the landscape.

## Outdoor Activities: Hiking trails, Pfeiffer Beach

Big Sur is more than just breathtaking scenery, it's also a haven for outdoor enthusiasts. The region's diverse terrain, from towering redwoods to rugged coastlines, provides ample opportunities for exploration and adventure. Whether you're a seasoned hiker or just looking for a peaceful escape, Big Sur's trails and beaches have something for you.

*Big Sur*

Hiking Trails

Big Sur's hiking trails take you through some of California's most scenic and diverse landscapes. Here are a few must-see routes that highlight the finest of what the area has to offer.

**Pfeiffer Falls walk:** This 2-mile round-trip walk in Pfeiffer Big Sur State Park leads to the scenic

Pfeiffer Falls across a dense redwood forest. The trail is well-maintained and suitable for hikers of all skill levels. As you walk among the towering redwoods, you'll feel a sense of peace and connection to nature that's hard to find elsewhere.

**Ewoldsen Trail:** Also in Julia Pfeiffer Burns State Park, the Ewoldsen Trail is a more challenging hike that offers stunning views of the coastline and the surrounding mountains. The 5-mile loop takes you through dense forests and along steep ridges, rewarding you with breathtaking vistas of the ocean and the rugged Big Sur landscape.

**Partington Cove walk:** This short but steep walk descends to a private cove where you may explore tidal pools and enjoy the serenity of a secret beach. The trail includes a tunnel that was used in the late 1800s to transport goods to ships anchored offshore. It's a fascinating glimpse into the history of the region.

**Andrew Molera State Park Trails:** This park offers a variety of trails that cater to different levels of hiking experience. The Bluffs Trail provides spectacular ocean views, while the River Trail takes you through grassy meadows and along the Big Sur River. The park's diverse ecosystems make it a great place for birdwatching and wildlife spotting.

## Pfeiffer Beach

A visit to Big Sur wouldn't be complete without a stop at Pfeiffer Beach, a hidden gem known for its unique purple sand and dramatic rock formations. Tucked away off the beaten path, Pfeiffer Beach is accessed via a narrow, winding road that leads you down to the shore. The effort to reach this secluded spot is well worth it.

As you arrive on the beach, you'll instantly notice the remarkable colour of the sand, which receives its purple tinge from manganese garnet particles washed down from the neighbouring slopes. The juxtaposition of the colourful sand against the turquoise waves of the Pacific is truly breathtaking.

One of the most recognizable aspects of Pfeiffer Beach is the enormous rock structure with a natural arch, known as Keyhole Rock. During the winter months, when the sun sets at the perfect angle, its rays reflect through the arch, producing a stunning light display that draws photographers from all over the globe.

Pfeiffer Beach is also an excellent place to explore tidal pools, picnic, or just relax and enjoy the scenery. The beach's distant position guarantees that it stays relatively uncrowded, enabling you to experience a feeling of privacy and serenity.

The trek from Monterey to Big Sur via the Pacific Coast Highway is a riveting excursion that shows the raw, untamed splendour of California's coastline. From the architectural beauty of Bixby Creek Bridge to the mesmerizing charm of McWay Falls, the panoramic delights of Big Sur never fail to inspire amazement and wonder. The region's hiking trails and hidden beaches offer endless opportunities for exploration and adventure, making it a paradise for outdoor enthusiasts and nature lovers alike.

As you cross this historic stretch of Highway 1, take the time to immerse yourself in the scenery, breathe in the fresh ocean air, and allow the beauty of Big Sur to wash over you. Whether you're gazing at the sunset from Bixby Creek Bridge, standing in amazement at McWay Falls, or discovering the hidden gems of Pfeiffer Beach, the charm of Big Sur is guaranteed to leave an unforgettable impact on your spirit.

### Iconic Stops: Point Lobos State Natural Reserve, Julia Pfeiffer Burns State Park

**Point Lobos State Natural Reserve**

As you begin your journey south from Monterey, your first major stop should be Point Lobos State Natural Reserve. Often referred to as the "crown jewel" of California's state park system, Point Lobos is a haven of natural beauty and biodiversity. The reserve has a rough shoreline, lush woods, and a diverse undersea ecology, making it an ideal destination for nature lovers and adventure enthusiasts.

Upon entering the reserve, you'll find a network of well-maintained trails that wind through diverse landscapes. The Cypress Grove Trail is a must-do, affording breathtaking vistas of the coastline and the renowned Monterey cypress trees that hang dangerously to the cliffs. As you stroll, keep an eye out for the rich wildlife that makes Point Lobos home, including sea otters, harbour seals, and a variety of seabirds.

For those interested in marine life, Point Lobos also provides outstanding chances for snorkelling and scuba diving. The underwater world here is brimming with life, from vibrant anemones and kelp forests to schools of fish and playful sea lions. Even if you remain on dry ground, Weston Beach's tidal pools are a veritable treasure trove of marine species, ideal for exploring with the family.

## Julia Pfeiffer Burns State Park

Julia Pfeiffer Burns State Park, located further south, is another hidden treasure along the Big Sur coastline. Named for a famous local pioneer lady, the park has some of California's most stunning landscapes. The main attraction, of course, is McWay Falls, but the park has a lot more to offer.

The Overlook Trail is a short, easy stroll with spectacular views of McWay Falls and the surrounding coastline. For a more immersive experience, the Ewoldsen Trail takes you on a loop through redwood groves and up to panoramic viewpoints overlooking the ocean. This hike is quite tough but well worth the effort for the sights it affords.

Julia Pfeiffer Burns State Park also has the remnants of the Waterfall House, which was constructed in the 1940s by Lathrop and Hélène Hooper Brown. Though the house is no longer standing, the terrace where it previously stood provides a beautiful view of the falls and cove below. It's a tranquil area that inspires meditation and appreciation of the natural beauty that surrounds you.

## Places to Eat and Stay in Big Sur

After a day of exploring the stunning landscapes and hiking trails, you'll want to find a place to relax and recharge. Big Sur has a variety of food and housing alternatives to suit a wide range of interests and budgets, assuring a pleasant visit.

### Dining at Big Sur

**Nepenthe:** Perched high on a rock, Nepenthe not only serves wonderful meals but also has some of the most stunning views in Big Sur. The menu features a mix of American and international dishes, with favourites like the Ambrosia Burger and the famous Nepenthe Triple Berry Pie. Enjoy your meal on the outdoor terrace, where you can take in the sweeping vistas of the coastline and the Pacific Ocean.

**Big Sur Bakery & Restaurant:** Located amid the redwoods, Big Sur Bakery is a delightful establishment noted for its wood-fired pizzas, freshly baked pastries, and locally sourced ingredients. The rustic environment and warm location make it ideal for a relaxing breakfast or supper. Don't miss the freshly made bread and seasonal treats.

**Sierra Mar:** Located at the luxurious Post Ranch Inn, Sierra Mar offers an upscale dining experience with a focus on farm-to-table cuisine. The restaurant's floor-to-ceiling windows give stunning views of the ocean, making it a great setting for a romantic evening. The menu varies periodically, presenting unique meals prepared from local ingredients.

**Deetjen's Big Sur Inn Restaurant:** For a taste of history and tradition, come to Deetjen's Big Sur Inn Restaurant. This historic inn, established in the 1930s, provides a warm and inviting ambiance with a cuisine that accentuates typical American comfort food. Enjoy a substantial breakfast or a comfortable meal by the fireplace in the rustic dining area.

## Where to Lodge in Big Sur

**Post Ranch Inn:** For those seeking elegance and tranquillity, Post Ranch Inn is the ultimate delight. This adults-only resort has beautiful suites with spectacular ocean or mountain views, private patios, and fireplaces. The infinity pools and spa treatments provide the ultimate relaxing experience, making it an ideal hideaway for couples.

**Ventana Big Sur:** Another deluxe choice, Ventana Big Sur has a variety of accommodations, including big suites and isolated glamping tents. The resort is situated on 160 acres of rolling hills and redwood trees, creating a tranquil and scenic atmosphere.

Guests may enjoy yoga sessions, guided hikes, and the resort's luxury spa.

**Big Sur River Inn:** For a more rustic and budget-friendly choice, the Big Sur River Inn provides lovely accommodations and cottages along the Big Sur River. The inn's laid-back attitude and riverfront setting make it a fantastic option for families and people wishing to connect with nature. Don't forget to rest in one of the Adirondack chairs put up in the river, which are ideal for cooling down on a hot day.

**Glen Oaks Big Sur:** This boutique hotel blends contemporary comfort and rustic charm. The tiny cabins and cottages are deliberately created using environmentally friendly materials and provide a serene refuge amid the redwoods. The property also has a community fire pit and access to gorgeous hiking paths.

**Deetjen's Big Sur Inn:** For those who like a historic and eccentric accommodation experience, Deetjen's Big Sur Inn is a unique choice. The inn's unique rooms are decorated with antiques and mementos, providing a nostalgic and welcoming environment. Staying at Deetjen's is like going back in time, with a delightful and genuine Big Sur experience.

The Pacific Coast Highway from Monterey to Big Sur is more than just a road trip; it provides an immersion into some of the world's most breathtaking vistas. From the renowned Bixby Creek Bridge to the majestic McWay Falls, as well as the hidden jewels of Point Lobos and Julia Pfeiffer Burns State Park, this route exemplifies California's coast's timeless splendour. So even if you wish to trek through old redwoods, find isolated coves, or just admire the panoramic vistas, Big Sur's natural beauties will leave an unforgettable mark on your heart and spirit. With a variety of food and housing choices to fit every taste and budget, your time in Big Sur will be as unforgettable as the trip itself.

# CHAPTER 6

## BIG SUR TO SAN LUIS OBISPO

Driving along the Pacific Coast Highway (PCH) from Big Sur to San Luis Obispo is a sensory delight. This scenery is a symphony of jagged coasts, where towering cliffs plunge precipitously into the roaring ocean, and the air is thick with the fragrance of salt and the sound of waves slamming against old rock.

As you leave the mysterious redwoods of Big Sur behind, Ragged Point provides a striking introduction to the region's wild splendour. Ragged Point, known as the **"Gateway to Big Sur,"** offers one of the most magnificent views along the Pacific Coast Highway. The tiny strip of land extends into the water, providing breathtaking panoramic coastline views. Here, you can stretch your legs and visit the Ragged Point Inn and Resort. The gardens, loaded with vivid blooms, contrast well against the background of the deep blue Pacific, making it an ideal location for a tranquil stroll or picnic.

The route continues southeast from Ragged Point, weaving through a landscape of cliffs and hidden bays. The ever-changing interplay of light and shadow on the cliffs and water below produces a captivating image that will compel you to grab your camera again and again.

A short journey farther down the PCH will take you to the Elephant Seal Rookery at Piedras Blancas. This distinct stretch of beach is home to one of nature's most spectacular spectacles: northern elephant seals. These giant marine creatures emerge from the water twice yearly to rest, molt, give birth, and breed on sandy beaches. The rookery is one of the few sites where you may see these creatures up close in their natural environment.

Standing on the observation platform, you'll see hundreds of elephant seals splayed over the beach, their big, blubbery bodies heaped on top of each other. The air is filled with the sound of their peculiar vocalizations, which include grunts, bellows, and snorts that reverberate throughout. Watching the seals interact is both entertaining and inspirational.

You'll observe the giant males, called bulls, fighting for supremacy, while the tiny ladies milk their pups and mingle with one another.
The rookery exemplifies nature's raw strength and beauty, providing a unique look into the life of these magnificent animals. Interpretive signs give useful information on seal behaviour, life cycles, and conservation efforts to preserve them. The experience is both instructive and extremely affecting, reminding us of the immense biodiversity found along the California coast.

## Historical Sites

**Hearst Castle:**
Continuing south, the PCH takes you to one of California's most recognizable historical sites, Hearst Castle. This sumptuous mansion, perched high on a hilltop in San Simeon, was designed

by media mogul **William Randolph Hearst** in collaboration with architect Julia Morgan. Construction started in 1919 and lasted almost three decades, culminating in a massive 165-room home that exemplifies the grandeur and extravagance of the early twentieth century.

As you approach the castle, the route swings over rolling hills populated with grazing cattle, providing views of the magnificent building in the distance. Upon arrival, a shuttle bus brings tourists up the steep, winding road to the estate, where the true beauty of Hearst Castle is revealed.

The villa is a remarkable combination of architectural forms, with Spanish, Moorish, and Mediterranean influences. The main building, Casa Grande, is tall and beautiful, with twin bell towers and a majestic façade. Inside, the castle is a treasure trove of art and antiquities gathered by Hearst from throughout the globe. The Assembly Room, with its beautifully carved oak ceiling and magnificent tapestries, sets the tone for the overall magnificence of the house.

A guided tour leads you through a succession of ornately adorned chambers, each more lavish than the last. The Refectory, the castle's main dining room, has a large table decked with sparkling cutlery and colourful mediaeval flags. The walls are adorned with rare artwork, and the space is illuminated by gigantic Gothic chandeliers, lending an air of old-world splendour.

One of the most remarkable aspects of Hearst Castle is its collection of outdoor areas, which are intended to take full use of the breathtaking natural surroundings. The Neptune Pool, with its sparkling blue water and ancient colonnades, is a defining feature of the estate's elegance. Nearby, the Roman Pool, an indoor swimming pool decorated with beautiful mosaic tiles and sculptures, provides a quieter but equally magnificent hideaway.

Aside from the main home, the estate has enormous gardens filled with vivid flowers, groomed hedges, and an astonishing collection of sculptures and fountains. The grounds are a calm retreat, ideal for a leisurely walk while admiring the spectacular views of the surrounding countryside and the Pacific Ocean.

Hearst Castle is more than simply a tribute to one man's riches and ambition; it's a doorway into another age. The estate reflects its owner's cultural goals and varied preferences, who wanted to construct a home that could serve as both a private refuge and a public spectacle.

Today, it serves as a testimony to the vision and workmanship of those who created it, as well as a reminder of California's historical and cultural past.

## Explore San Luis Obispo: Mission San Luis Obispo, Downtown SLO

As you travel south along the Pacific Coast Highway, your next stop is the picturesque town of **San Luis Obispo (SLO).** San Luis Obispo, located in the center of the Central Coast, has a lovely combination of history, culture, and small-town charm that entices travellers to discover its riches.

**Mission Santa Luis Obispo:**
San Luis Obispo's cultural past includes Mission San Luis Obispo de Tolosa, one of California's ancient Spanish missions. Father Junipero Serra founded the mission in 1772, and it played an important part in California's colonization and the propagation of Christianity among the Native American Chumash.

The mission's unique adobe architecture and quiet gardens provide a peaceful respite from the busy town core. Stepping into the mission grounds transports you back to a period of Spanish colonial dominance. The massive façade of the mission church and surrounding buildings are embellished with exquisite decorations and whitewashed walls that represent the region's rich heritage.

Inside the mission church, the air is cold and silent, interrupted only by the gentle glow of sunshine streaming through stained glass windows. The inside is filled with classic Spanish colonial artwork, such as beautiful altars, saint statues, and bright murals depicting biblical stories and local history.

Outside, the mission's gardens provide a tranquil haven among the bustling activity of downtown San Luis Obispo. Fragrant roses blossom among native flora, and shady walkways entice visitors to explore and ponder. The mission is still an operating parish today, acting as both a place of prayer and a living museum preserving California's Spanish colonial legacy.

**Downtown SLO:**

After seeing Mission San Luis Obispo, take a walk around Downtown SLO, a thriving center of shops, restaurants, and historic sites. The core of downtown is concentrated on Higuera Street, where tree-lined pathways and Victorian-era buildings provide a friendly ambiance.

Downtown SLO is a sanctuary for art lovers, with galleries displaying works by both local and international artists. You may stroll through quirky businesses selling anything from handcrafted jewelry to vintage apparel and one-of-a-kind souvenirs that encapsulate the essence of the Central Coast.

For history aficionados, buildings like the Fremont Theater and the San Luis Obispo County Historical Museum provide insight into the region's rich history. The Fremont Theater, with its distinctive Art Deco sign, is a hallmark of San Luis Obispo's thriving entertainment industry, hosting a range of live acts and film screenings all year.

### Dining and Accommodations in San Luis Obispo

San Luis Obispo's culinary culture reflects its agricultural history and seaside surroundings, with a wide range of eating choices emphasizing fresh, locally produced foods and unique tastes. Whether you're looking for farm-to-table cooking, seafood delights, or cuisine, SLO has it all.

Many San Luis Obispo restaurants take pride in their commitment to sustainability and supporting local farmers and fishermen. There are plenty of gastronomic treats to uncover, ranging from intimate cafés providing handmade coffee and pastries to upmarket restaurants offering fine dining experiences.

After a day of exploring, San Luis Obispo has a variety of lodgings to fit any traveller's needs and budget. Downtown hotels and boutique inns give easy access to activities and restaurants, whilst lovely bed-and-breakfasts provide a more private and customized experience. For those looking for a more natural vacation, surrounding resorts and lodges provide tranquil locations surrounded by rolling hills or ocean panoramas.

Whether you want to reside in a historic inn with period furnishings or in a contemporary hotel with excellent facilities, San Luis Obispo's lodgings guarantee comfort and hospitality that will improve your Central Coast experience.

Also, exploring San Luis Obispo and its surroundings along the Pacific Coast Highway is an adventure full of discovery and joy. From the historic Mission San Luis Obispo and bustling Downtown SLO to the delectable eating choices and welcoming hotels, this stretch of the PCH provides a rich tapestry of experiences that highlight California's cultural legacy and natural beauty.

Hence, the Pacific Coast Highway from Big Sur to San Luis Obispo is an unforgettable trip through California's natural beauty and cultural legacy. From the rocky cliffs and beautiful beaches of Ragged Point and the Elephant Seal Rookery to the opulent beauty of Hearst Castle.
Therefore, as you continue your journey down the Pacific Coast Highway, take the time to experience the views, tastes, and history that distinguish San Luis Obispo. Whether you're attracted to the peacefulness of the mission

gardens, the bustling vitality of downtown streets, or the gastronomic pleasures that lie around every corner, San Luis Obispo welcomes you and encourages you to have memorable experiences along this renowned coastal path.

# CHAPTER 7

## SAN LUIS OBISPO TO SANTA BARBARA

As you leave the rolling hills of San Luis Obispo and go south on the Pacific Coast Highway, you'll discover a stretch of California coastline that perfectly mixes natural beauty with small charm. This is where you'll discover Pismo Beach and Avila Beach, two picturesque settlements that embody coastal life.

**Pismo Beach:**

Pismo Beach is a classic California beach town famed for its vast sandy beaches, landmark pier, and relaxed vibe. As you reach Pismo Beach, the sight of the Pacific Ocean shimmering in the sun will take your breath away. Pismo Pier, the town's primary attraction, spreads out into the ocean, providing breathtaking views of the coastline and the ideal location for a leisurely walk or fishing.

Surfers, swimmers, and sunbathers may all enjoy the beach. The waves here are great for surfing, and you'll see both locals and tourists riding the swells. If you want to try your hand at surfing, various surf schools along the beach provide training for all ability levels. For those who prefer to keep dry, the beach is ideal for playing volleyball, making sandcastles, or just resting with a good book.

Pismo Beach isn't just about the water. The town is well-known for its lovely downtown area, which has a variety of shops, restaurants, and cafés. Take a trip along Price Street and you'll come across fascinating businesses selling anything from beachwear to handcrafted jewelry. When hunger hits, the local restaurants provide a variety of excellent selections, including fresh seafood and typical American meals. Make sure to taste the clam chowder at Splash Cafe, a local staple that has been serving this creamy delicacy for decades.

**Avila Beach:**

Avila Beach, a lesser-known but enchanting resort, is just a short drive away from Pismo Beach. Avila Beach, located in a secluded inlet, provides a more private and serene experience than its crowded neighbour. The trip to Avila Beach winds past beautiful vineyards and rolling hills, preparing you for the magnificence that awaits.

Avila Beach is smaller and more private, making it ideal for a peaceful day by the ocean. The calm waves and warm, sun-drenched beaches make this a perfect spot for families and people wishing to unwind. The beachside promenade is packed with attractive shops and restaurants, offering everything from a simple ice cream cone to a gourmet lunch with an ocean view.

The Avila Hot Springs, one of Avila Beach's distinctive attractions, offers guests the opportunity to bathe in natural mineral hot springs that have been luring people for over a century. The therapeutic waters are claimed to have restorative characteristics, making it the ideal place to relax after a day of touring.

For a little adventure, rent a kayak or paddleboard and explore the tranquil waters of San Luis Obispo Bay. The adjacent Avila Beach Golf Resort is a wonderful course with breathtaking ocean views, ideal for a relaxed game of golf. Avila Beach strikes the ideal combination of relaxation and activity.

**Wine Country: Edna , Paso Robles.**

As you travel from San Luis Obispo to Santa Barbara, you'll pass through some of California's most renowned wine regions. The Edna Valley and Paso Robles districts are well-known for their vineyards and wineries, providing a lovely diversion for both wine lovers and casual tourists.

**Edna Valley:**

Edna Valley, only a few miles inland from Pismo Beach, is a wine enthusiast's dream. The area is well-known for its cool-climate varieties, especially Chardonnay and Pinot Noir. The closeness to the seaside creates a distinct environment that produces wines with high acidity and diverse flavours.

The trip through Edna Valley is breathtaking, with vineyards spanning as far as the eye can see, dotted with rolling hills and charming farmhouses. Many of the vineyards are family-owned, providing tourists with a pleasant and inviting ambiance. Tastings are frequently small gatherings where you may learn about the winemaking process firsthand from the folks who make the wines.

Tolosa Winery is a must-see winery in Edna Valley, combining cutting-edge technology with traditional winemaking processes to create superb wines. Their tasting facility has panoramic views of the neighbouring vineyards, giving a peaceful background while you try their wines. Another hidden treasure is Edna Valley Vineyard, which is noted for its magnificent setting and excellent wines. A visit here is a sensory treat, from the stunning gardens to the delectable wines.

**Paso Robles:**

Paso Robles, located farther inland, offers a unique but equally delightful wine experience. This area is known for its robust red wines, especially Zinfandel, Cabernet Sauvignon, and Rhône varietals. The warm temperature and diversified geography of Paso Robles produce wines with rich, powerful characteristics.

Paso Robles is home to over 200 wineries, each with its distinct charm. Whether you're an experienced oenophile or a complete newbie, there's something for everyone. Paso Robles' terrain is varied, ranging from rolling vineyards to oak-studded hills, making it a perfect backdrop for wine tasting.

Justin Vineyards & Winery is one of Paso Robles' most notable wineries, noted for its world-class Bordeaux-style blends. The house is a destination in and of itself, complete with magnificent gardens, a gourmet restaurant, and elegant rooms. A tasting at Justin is a complete experience that highlights the finest of Paso Robles winemaking.

Another must-see is **Tablas Creek Vineyard**, which was a pioneer of Rhône varietals in California. The winery was founded as a collaboration with Château de Beaucastel in

France, introducing traditional Rhône winemaking practices to the area. The result is a collection of wines that are both unique and well-regarded.

Beyond the vineyards, Paso Robles has a pleasant downtown area with a variety of shops, galleries, and restaurants. The ancient downtown square, with its charming streets and pleasant ambiance, is an excellent site to explore. Make sure to come to one of the numerous wine festivals conducted throughout the year, where you may try a variety of local wines while enjoying the festive atmosphere.

**Journey's End: Santa Barbara**

As you leave wine country and go south on the Pacific Coast Highway, you'll arrive at Santa Barbara, sometimes known as the **"American Riviera"**. Santa Barbara, with its Mediterranean temperature, beautiful beaches and Spanish-style architecture, is an appropriate place to end this portion of your vacation. The city has the right balance of natural beauty and cultural diversity, making it a wonderful place to unwind and reflect on your trip experiences.

In Santa Barbara, you may walk along State Street, see the historic Mission Santa Barbara, or just relax on the lovely beaches. The city's thriving cultural scene, world-class food, and elegant hotels make for an ideal conclusion to your voyage from San Luis Obispo.

As you journey from San Luis Obispo to Santa Barbara, the gorgeous communities of Pismo Beach and Avila Beach, as well as the famed wine areas of Edna Valley and Paso Robles, provide a diverse range of experiences. Each stop along the journey has its distinct charm, resulting in memories that will last long after you leave the Pacific Coast Highway behind.

### Explore Santa Barbara
*(Stearns Wharf, Santa Barbara Mission)*

As you approach Santa Barbara, the terrain shifts slowly, exposing a city where mountains meet the sea. This lovely transition sets the setting for seeing some of Santa Barbara's most famous sites.

**Stearns Wharf:**

Stearns Wharf, situated at the end of State Street, is one of Santa Barbara's most renowned attractions. Built-in 1872, it is California's oldest operational wharf and provides a nostalgic peek into the city's nautical history. As you stroll over the wooden planks, you can practically hear echoes of the wharf's former life as a busy shopping center.

Stearns Wharf is now a popular site for both residents and tourists. The views from the wharf are stunning, with the Santa Ynez Mountains towering majestically in the backdrop and the dazzling Pacific Ocean reaching out in front. Take your time browsing the stores and boutiques that line the waterfront, which sell everything from souvenirs to local art.

Dining at Stearns Wharf is a delight, with many eateries serving up fresh seafood and breathtaking ocean views. One of the attractions is the Santa Barbara Shellfish Company, where you may eat freshly caught shellfish and watch the sunset over the lake. If you're looking for something sweet, don't miss Mother Stearns Candy Company, a quaint establishment that serves handcrafted fudge and traditional sweets.

For a little adventure, rent a kayak or paddleboard at the dock and explore the shoreline from the sea. The tranquil waters of Santa Barbara Harbor are ideal for kayaking, providing a unique view of the city and its surroundings. Alternatively, take a trip on the lovely Lil' Toot water taxi, which transports tourists between Stearns Wharf and Santa Barbara Harbor.

**Santa Barbara Mission:**

No trip to Santa Barbara is complete without seeing the Santa Barbara Mission, sometimes known as the "Queen of the Missions." This historic site, founded by the Spanish Franciscans in 1786, exemplifies the city's rich cultural past. The mission's spectacular design, with its twin bell towers and gorgeous gardens, represents Santa Barbara's mix of Spanish and Native American elements.

The mission remains a functioning parish, and visitors are invited to attend mass or just tour the grounds. The on-site museum provides an intriguing glimpse into the mission's history and the individuals who lived and served there. The museum's displays contain early mission relics such as religious objects, Native American implements, and historical papers.

The mission's gardens are a feature, displaying a variety of flora grown by the early settlers. The calm location, with its lush vegetation and bright flowers, offers a quiet respite from the hustle and bustle of the city. Don't miss the Mission Cemetery, where many early settlers, including

Native Americans and Spanish colonists, are buried.

## Where to Eat and Stay in Santa Barbara

Santa Barbara's food scene and lodging alternatives are just as broad and dynamic as the city itself. From exquisite restaurants to informal cafes, and luxurious hotels to lovely bed & breakfasts, Santa Barbara has something for everyone's taste and budget.

### Where To Eat

Santa Barbara is a foodie's dream, with a variety of eating choices reflecting the city's broad cultural influences and seaside wealth.

- **The Lark:** Located in the heart of the Funk Zone, The Lark provides a farm-to-table dining experience that highlights the greatest Central Coast products. The menu offers a range of sharing platters, including fresh seafood, locally produced meats, and veggies. The outside patio, with its glittering lights and community tables, offers a warm and welcoming ambiance.

- **Brophy Bros:** For seafood enthusiasts, Brophy Bros. is a must-see. This popular diner on Santa Barbara Harbor is well-known for its delicious seafood and vibrant environment. Enjoy a cup of their famed clam chowder or a dish of freshly shucked oysters while seeing the breathtaking waterfront views.

- **Santa Barbara Public Market:** If you're seeking diversity, visit the Santa Barbara Public Market. This bustling market has a variety of artisanal food sellers selling anything from sushi and gourmet burgers to craft beer and wine. It's the ideal setting for a quick snack or a leisurely lunch with friends.

Where to stay

Santa Barbara has a wide choice of hotels to accommodate any tourist, from opulent resorts to modest inns.

- **The Ritz-Carlton Bacara, Santa Barbara:** The Ritz-Carlton Bacara provides a genuinely opulent experience with breathtaking ocean views, world-class facilities, and exceptional service. The resort offers tastefully decorated suites, a variety of dining choices, a magnificent spa, and direct access to a gorgeous beach. It's the ideal spot to relax and take in the splendour of the California coast.

**-The Simpson House Inn:** If you prefer a more personal environment, the Simpson House Inn provides a delightful bed-and-breakfast experience in the center of Santa Barbara. This ancient Victorian mansion has tastefully appointed rooms, gorgeous grounds, and attentive service. Each morning, enjoy a gourmet breakfast, followed by free wine and cheese in the evening.

**-Hotel Milos:** Milo, located only feet from the beach, provides a relaxing beachfront ambiance with spacious rooms and courteous service. The hotel's colourful, coastal-inspired decor and accessible location make it a popular option for those seeking to discover the best of Santa Barbara.

As your trip down the Pacific Coast Highway comes to a close in Santa Barbara, the city's distinct combination of natural beauty, rich history, and lively culture gives an appropriate conclusion to your excursion. From the picturesque settlements of Pismo Beach and Avila Beach to the undulating vineyards of Edna Valley and Paso Robles, and eventually to the seaside elegance of Santa Barbara, this length of the PCH provides an amazing journey. Each stop along the route lends its own unique flavour to the voyage, resulting in a tapestry of memories that will last long after you've left the road behind.

# CHAPTER 8

# SANTA BARBARA TO LOS ANGELES

**Coastal Gems: Ventura and Malibu**

As you leave the lovely city of Santa Barbara, where Spanish Colonial Revival architecture blends with palm-lined beaches, the Pacific Coast Highway (PCH) continues to be a sensory delight. The journey south is a patchwork of stunning coasts, quaint tiny villages, and the alluring sweep of the Pacific Ocean.

**Ventura:**

The first destination on the schedule is Ventura, a city that frequently goes unnoticed but provides a plethora of experiences for those who pause to explore. Ventura, once known as San Buenaventura, combines historic elegance with contemporary energy. The downtown district, which is filled with Mission-style buildings, welcomes you to meander through its streets and explore a variety of boutique stores, cafés, and art galleries. Don't miss the San Buenaventura Mission, which was established in 1782 and allows you to journey back in time and reflect on California's Spanish heritage.

Ventura Harbor Village is a must-see for those who like the outdoors. You may go on an adventure at Channel Islands National Park from here. The Channel Islands, sometimes known as the "Galápagos of North America," are home to varied fauna and rare plant species. Whether you prefer to kayak through sea caves, trek difficult paths, or dive in the crystal-clear seas, the islands guarantee an amazing experience.

Back on the mainland, Ventura's beaches are similarly appealing. Surfer's Point, as the name implies, is a surfers' paradise, and the neighbouring promenade is ideal for a leisurely bike ride or sunset walk. The coastal wind, mixed with the city's laid-back ethos, results in a refreshing and calm environment.

**Malibu:**

Continuing south, the PCH leads to Malibu, a city known for its surf culture, celebrity homes, and beautiful beaches. This 21-mile strip of paradise has earned its reputation for good reason. The trip itself is breathtaking, with the Santa Monica Mountains rising to your left and the broad Pacific Ocean to your right.

One of the first stops in Malibu should be **Zuma Beach**. This large sandy beach is ideal for a day of sunbathing, beach volleyball, or simply watching the waves roll in. Zuma's vast open spaces and immaculate conditions make it a popular destination for both locals and visitors.

El Matador State Beach provides a more secluded experience with dramatic cliffs, sea caves, and rock formations. It's a photographer's dream and a lovely area for exploring tidal pools or having a picnic while watching the sunset.

No visit to Malibu is complete without a stop at the Malibu Pier. This ancient site offers breathtaking ocean views and the opportunity to see local fishermen in action. Malibu Farm Restaurant, located next to the pier, serves farm-to-table cuisine against a stunning background. Enjoy fresh, organic cuisine while taking in the breathtaking seaside views.

As you travel through Malibu, you'll see various famous houses and private estates nestled away in the hills and along the beach. While these houses are not open to the public, they contribute to Malibu's charm and mystery, cementing its reputation as a playground for the wealthy and famous.

### Iconic LA Landmarks:
*(Santa Monica Pier, Venice Beach, and Hollywood)*

As the PCH continues south, it takes you into the busy core of Los Angeles. The transition from the tranquil beaches of Ventura and Malibu to the vibrant cityscape of LA is both thrilling and exhilarating.

**Santa Monica Pier:**

Santa Monica Pier is a quintessential California experience. This iconic landmark, with its Ferris wheel and roller coaster, is a beacon of nostalgia and fun. The pier, which has been a popular meeting spot for over a century, features a carnival-like ambiance with amusement park rides, arcade games, and vibrant street performers.

For a fresh viewpoint, take a walk along the pier at sunset. The golden colours of the setting sun shed a lovely light over the water, producing a stunning backdrop that's excellent for photography. The nearby Santa Monica State Beach, with its wide sandy shores, is ideal for swimming or playing beach volleyball.

Don't forget to explore the Santa Monica area. The third area Promenade is a bustling pedestrian area with stores, restaurants, and entertainment. Whether you're seeking high-end apparel, one-of-a-kind souvenirs, or a fantastic lunch, this lively district offers it all.

**Venice Beach:**

Just a short drive from Santa Monica, Venice Beach offers a sharp contrast with its unique and bohemian attitude. Known for its vibrant promenade, Venice is a feast for the senses. Street entertainers, sellers, and artists line the promenade, presenting a kaleidoscope of sights and sounds.

Muscle Beach, a historic outdoor gym, is a focal point where bodybuilders and fitness fanatics show off their power and expertise. The local skate park draws skateboarders from all around, showing incredible feats and acrobatics.

The Venice Canals, a hidden gem inspired by Italy's Venice, offer a tranquil respite from the busy boardwalk. Stroll around the small canals, crossing picturesque footbridges, and admiring the modest cottages that border them. It's a tranquil and picturesque location that feels worlds apart from the bustling beach scene.

For food and shopping, Abbot Kinney Boulevard is a must-see. This trendy street is lined with boutique shops, gourmet restaurants, and chic cafés. Whether you're looking for a gourmet meal or a quick bite, the culinary options here are varied and innovative.

**Hollywood:**

No trip to Los Angeles is complete without visiting Hollywood, the entertainment industry's epicenter. As you leave the coast and head inland, you'll be immersed in the glitz and glamour that define this iconic neighbourhood.

The Hollywood Walk of Fame, with its star-studded sidewalks, commemorates the rich history of film and television. As you stroll down Hollywood Boulevard, you'll discover the names of innumerable personalities who have made their impact on the business. Don't miss the TCL Chinese Theatre, which features the handprints and footprints of famous actors and directors.

To get a panoramic view of the city, visit the Griffith Observatory. Perched on the southern slope of Mount Hollywood, the observatory offers breathtaking views of Los Angeles, the Hollywood Sign, and the surrounding mountains. It's a perfect spot for both stargazing and city gazing.

The Hollywood Sign, an emblem of the entertainment industry, can be seen from several vantage points throughout the city. Hiking one of Griffith Park's paths will provide a closer view. The hike not only offers breathtaking views but also a sense of accomplishment as you approach the iconic landmark.

As you tour Hollywood, you'll also meet a wealth of museums, theaters, and historic landmarks that honour the city's movie legacy. The Hollywood Museum, situated in the historic Max Factor Building, presents intriguing exhibitions on the history of cinema and television.

Thus, the Pacific Coast Highway between Santa Barbara and Los Angeles combines quiet seaside scenery with lively metropolitan activity. Every stop along the road, from the modest beauty of Ventura to the dazzling appeal of Hollywood, provides a unique view into Southern California's rich journey.

## The Best Neighbourhoods

**Beverly Hills**

Beverly Hills embodies opulence, elegance, and a taste of the good life. This recognizable area is known for its luxurious residences, world-class shopping, and celebrity sightings. As you drive through its tree-lined streets, you'll encounter some of the most beautiful and expensive homes in the world.

Rodeo Drive is the heart of the Beverly Hills shopping district. This world-famous boulevard is dotted with luxury shops and flagship stores from the likes of Chanel, Gucci, and Louis Vuitton. Even if you're not expecting to make a purchase, wandering along Rodeo Drive is an experience in itself. The window displays are like art pieces, each one more magnificent than the previous one.

Beyond shopping, Beverly Hills offers cultural attractions such as the Beverly Hills Hotel, often called the "Pink Palace," and the Greystone Mansion and Park, a historic estate with beautiful gardens and panoramic views of the city. For a touch of elegance, try taking a guided tour of the neighbourhood to visit the houses of Hollywood's elite and hear intriguing anecdotes about the area's famous history.

**Downtown Los Angeles:**

Downtown Los Angeles (DTLA) has undergone significant transformations in recent years, emerging as a thriving center of culture, history, and innovation. The neighbourhood combines architectural styles, gastronomic pleasures, and creative expression.

Begin your trip with the historic Union Station, an architectural marvel that serves as Los Angeles' major train station. From here, you may walk to Olvera Street, a lively Mexican market that honours LA's Latino roots. The colourful stalls, traditional foods, and mariachi music make for an exciting and immersive cultural experience.

The Broad Museum, with its striking contemporary architecture, houses an impressive collection of postwar and contemporary art. Nearby, the Walt Disney Concert Hall, created by Frank Gehry, is an architectural marvel that houses the Los Angeles Philharmonic. Its stainless steel contours and dynamic design make it a must-see destination.

DTLA is also known for its culinary scene, which includes a wide variety of dining options that reflect the city's multicultural population. The Grand Central Market is a food lover's heaven, providing everything from tacos and ramen to artisanal coffee and gourmet burgers. For a more refined dining experience, head to one of the rooftop bars and restaurants that provide stunning views of the city skyline.

**Griffith Park:**

Griffith Park, one of North America's largest urban parks, is a haven of natural beauty and outdoor adventure located in the heart of Los Angeles. The park, which spans over 4,000 acres, offers a variety of activities for both nature enthusiasts and families.

The Griffith Observatory is a feature of the park, affording amazing views of Los Angeles and the famed Hollywood Sign. The observatory itself offers intriguing displays on space and astronomy, and its position on the southern slope of Mount Hollywood makes it a perfect area for stargazing.

For those who prefer hiking, Griffith Park offers various pathways that appeal to all levels of expertise. The trip to the Hollywood Sign is very popular, offering a strenuous journey with breathtaking views of the city and the Pacific Ocean.

Another family-friendly destination is the Los Angeles Zoo and Botanical Gardens, which are situated in Griffith Park. The zoo has a wide assortment of animals from throughout the globe, while the botanical gardens provide a calm escape with stunning plant displays.

### Dining and Accommodations in Los Angeles

Los Angeles is a culinary powerhouse, with a wide range of eating choices reflecting its broad cultural mix. From Michelin-starred restaurants to innovative food trucks, the city's culinary culture is as diverse as it is delectable.

## Dining in Los Angeles

Providence on **Melrose Avenue** is a high-end eating option. This Michelin-starred restaurant is famous for its superb seafood dishes and outstanding service. Chef Michael Cimarusti's tasting menu is a voyage through the greatest ingredients and culinary methods.

**Bestia,** situated in the Arts District, is a favourite with residents and travellers alike. This Italian restaurant is noted for its homemade charcuterie, wood-fired pizzas, and creative pasta dishes. The industrial-chic environment enhances the colourful and active vibe.

For a taste of LA's legendary street cuisine, travel to **Grand Central Market** or one of the numerous food truck gatherings throughout the city. You may have tacos from Guerilla Tacos,

Korean BBQ from Kogi BBQ and a variety of other ethnic cuisines.

If you're looking for something different, **n/naka** provides an unforgettable kaiseki experience. Chef Niki Nakayama prepares elaborate multi-course feasts that honour the creativity and heritage of Japanese cuisine. Reservations are required since this tiny eatery is in great demand.

## Accommodation in Los Angeles

Los Angeles has a diverse choice of hotel alternatives to fit any budget or desire. For a deluxe stay, look into the **Beverly Hills Hotel** or **the Four Seasons Hotel** Los Angeles in Beverly Hills. These legendary hotels provide sumptuous accommodations, first-rate services, and a touch of Hollywood glamour.

**The Ace Hotel** is a hip alternative in Downtown Los Angeles, featuring a rooftop pool and bar that offers panoramic city views. The hotel's historic architecture and sophisticated decor make it a favourite option among creatives.

For those seeking a seaside experience, the Shutters on the Beach in Santa Monica offers a classic Southern California ambiance. This exquisite hotel has breathtaking ocean views, direct beach access, and a tranquil coastal setting.

If you want a more boutique experience, the **Kimpton La Peer Hotel** in West Hollywood is a stylish and modern choice. Its prominent position in the Design District makes it perfect for visiting the neighbourhood's art galleries, shopping, and eateries.

From the opulence of Beverly Hills to the cultural excitement of Downtown LA and the natural beauty of Griffith Park, Los Angeles has a broad range of communities, each telling its narrative. Combined with its world-class food and lodging choices, the city offers visitors an immersive and unique experience. As you visit this vibrant city, you'll learn how LA encapsulates the spirit of Southern California life, combining the glitter of Hollywood with the varied appeal of its many neighbourhoods.

# CHAPTER 9

# LOS ANGELES TO ORANGE COUNTY

The Pacific Coast Highway (PCH) from Los Angeles to Orange County presents a true Californian dreamscape, with sun-soaked beaches, creative enclaves, and world-renowned family attractions. This chapter allows you to discover the colourful coastal communities of Huntington Beach, Newport Beach, and Laguna Beach, each with its distinct charm and intrigue.

**Huntington Beach:**

As you travel south from Los Angeles, your first stop should be Huntington Beach, often known as "Surf City USA." This legendary surf town is a paradise for wave riders, sunbathers, and beachcombers alike. Huntington Beach is the perfect beach resort, with over eight miles of beautiful beachfront.

Huntington Beach's busy pier, which extends 1,850 feet into the Pacific Ocean, is the city's heart. The pier is an ideal location for a leisurely walk, with panoramic views of the ocean and the busy city behind you. Surfers may be seen slicing the waves below at any time of day, demonstrating the city's strong surf culture. Don't miss the International Surfing Museum, a tiny but intriguing collection of surf history and memorabilia that honours luminaries like Duke Kahanamoku and local hero Corky Carroll.

For individuals who want to try surfing for themselves, various surf schools provide training for all skill levels. The beach also hosts the annual U.S. The Open of Surfing is the world's greatest surf championship, transforming the region into a bustling celebration of sports, music, and art.

**Newport Beach**

Continuing south on the PCH, you'll arrive at Newport Beach, a city known for its coastal beauty and nautical appeal. Newport Beach is a water enthusiast's paradise, with a beautiful harbour packed with yachts, sailboats, and attractive waterfront residences.

Balboa Island, accessible by a short boat trip or bridge, is a must-see. This small island is reminiscent of old-time America, with scenic lanes dotted with lovely homes, boutique stores, and excellent cafes. Indulge in the famed Balboa Bar or Frozen Banana, a local favourite.

Newport Beach's shoreline is similarly appealing. Newport Beach Municipal Beach, sometimes known as "Newport Beach," is a vast expanse of sand ideal for sunbathing, beach volleyball, and swimming. The beach is anchored by the historic Newport Pier, which is renowned for fishing and sunset viewing.

Fashion Island, an upmarket open-air retail mall, provides a new kind of seaside experience. Here, you may enjoy high-end shopping, great restaurants, and stunning views of the Pacific

Ocean. Whether you're touring the marina, taking a harbour cruise, or eating at one of the numerous waterfront restaurants, Newport Beach personifies the traditional California coastal lifestyle.

**Laguna Beach:**

Laguna Beach, located farther down the PCH, is well-known for its natural beauty and active arts scene. Laguna Beach, nestled between cliffs and the ocean, provides some of California's most magnificent coastal landscapes.

Laguna Beach's Main Beach, with its renowned lifeguard tower and boardwalk, is popular with both residents and tourists. The beach is ideal for swimming, sunbathing, and beach volleyball. The tidal pools at the northern and southern extremities of the beach are an excellent place to see marine life up close.

It is deeply rooted in the arts. Throughout the year, the city holds several art events, including the Sawdust Art Festival, the Festival of Arts, and the Pageant of the Masters, where art is brought to life in beautifully prepared tableau vivant. Stroll around the city's central district, where you'll discover a profusion of galleries displaying works by local and international artists.

Laguna Beach also has a network of hiking paths that provide spectacular views of the ocean and valleys. The Laguna Coast Wilderness Park is an excellent spot to see the region's natural splendour, with paths that snake through oak and sycamore trees, coastal sage scrub, and rocky bluffs.

## Family Attractions:

No trip to Orange County is complete without seeing the area's world-famous family attractions. **Disneyland and Knott's Berry Farm,** two classic theme parks that have entertained tourists for decades, are just a short drive inland from the PCH.

**Disneyland:**

Disneyland, located in Anaheim, is a magical place where dreams come true. Disneyland Park, which opened in 1955, was the first Disney theme park and was designed under Walt Disney's supervision. The park is organised into themed areas, with each having its own set of activities, events, and experiences.

Main Street, U.S.A. transports tourists to small-town America in the early twentieth century, complete with lovely stores and cafés. Adventureland offers exciting exploits, whilst Frontierland transports you back to the Wild West. Fantasyland brings iconic Disney characters and tales to life, while Tomorrowland's sci-fi attractions provide visitors with a look into the future.

Disneyland is well-known for its renowned rides and attractions, including Space Mountain, Pirates of the Caribbean, and the Haunted

Mansion. The park also has contemporary attractions such as Star Wars: Galaxy's Edge, where you can immerse yourself in the Star Wars world, pilot the Millennium Falcon, and meet your favourite characters from the movie.

Disneyland's evening entertainment is renowned, including breathtaking fireworks, parades, and light displays that captivate guests of all ages. Disneyland is an unforgettable experience, whether you meet Mickey Mouse, on a classic Disney ride, or witness a stunning parade.

**Knott's Berry Farm:**

Knott's Berry Farm, located only a few miles from Disneyland in Buena Park, provides a unique theme park experience that combines exhilarating rides with a rich historical backdrop. What started as a berry farm and roadside stand in the 1920s has evolved into one of California's most popular amusement parks.

Ghost Town, the center of Knott's Berry Farm, evokes the mood of the Old West with its wooden structures, costumed performers, and live performances. You may pan for gold, see blacksmith demonstrations, and enjoy the Wild West Stunt Show.

Knott's Berry Farm has a fantastic collection of roller coasters and attractions for thrill seekers. From the stomach-churning drops of Xcelerator and the inversions of Silver Bullet to the traditional thrills of the Timber Mountain Log Ride, there is something for everyone. The park also has Camp Snoopy, a Peanuts-themed section for children that includes moderate rides and interactive activities.

It is also known for its boysenberry-inspired delicacies. The annual Boysenberry Festival celebrates the park's agricultural history by showcasing a range of boysenberry-flavoured delicacies, including pies, jams, savoury meals, and artisan drinks.

## Dining and Shopping in Orange County

Orange County is known for more than just its stunning beaches and exhilarating activities, it is also a gourmet and shopping paradise. There is something for everyone, from gourmet restaurants to casual seaside eateries, as well as luxury boutiques and eccentric local stores.

### Dining in Orange County

**Huntington Beach:**
Huntington Beach has a diverse food scene that caters to all tastes. Duke's Huntington Beach is a popular spot for a typical beachside dining experience. This restaurant, named after a renowned surfer Duke Kahanamoku, offers Hawaiian-inspired cuisine and breathtaking ocean views. Don't miss their legendary Hula Pie for dessert.

For seafood aficionados, **the Fish Camp** on PCH offers a relaxed ambiance and a menu that includes fresh catches of the day, clam chowder, and oysters. Another excellent choice is Pacific Hideaway, which serves a blend of Asian, Latin American and Californian dishes in a bright, surf-inspired environment.

**Newport Beach:**

Newport Beach is recognized for its premium eating scene, which includes a variety of high-end restaurants and informal cafes. Nobu Newport Beach, situated on the Lido Peninsula, provides a world-class Japanese-Peruvian dining experience including outstanding sushi and seafood specialties.

For an outstanding waterfront dining experience, go to The Cannery Seafood of the Pacific. This restaurant, located in a historic structure, serves fresh seafood, and steaks, and has a beautiful view of Newport Harbor. If you prefer a more informal atmosphere, Bear Flag Fish Co. on the Balboa Peninsula serves fresh poke bowls, fish tacos, and seafood salads.

**Laguna Beach:**

Laguna Beach's food scene is as broad and lively as its artistic community. The Deck on Laguna Beach is a well-known restaurant that serves meals directly on the beach. Enjoy ahi poke, lobster tacos, and their legendary margaritas while watching the surf crash.

Studio at Montage Laguna Beach offers a unique culinary experience. This fine-dining restaurant serves seasonal, garden-to-table food with an emphasis on local products, all against the background of the Pacific Ocean. Another must-see is Nick's Laguna Beach, which serves American classics and unique drinks.

## Shop in Orange County

**Fashion Island:**
Fashion Island in Newport Beach is a top shopping destination with a mix of premium goods, specialized shops, and excellent restaurants. This open-air shopping area has high-end retailers such as Neiman Marcus, Bloomingdale's, and Nordstrom, as well as

distinctive local enterprises. Stroll through beautifully manicured courtyards, dine al fresco, and see the breathtaking views of the Pacific Ocean.

**South Coast Plaza:**

South Shore Plaza, located in Costa Mesa and just a short drive from the shore, is one of the biggest and most prominent shopping malls in the United States. It's a fashionista's dream, with over 250 boutiques including Chanel, Gucci, Louis Vuitton, and other brands. The mall also has a variety of food choices, including upmarket restaurants and informal cafés, making it ideal for a full day of shopping and dining.

**Laguna Beach:**

Laguna Beach's diverse mix of art galleries, boutiques, and specialized stores provide for a one-of-a-kind shopping experience. Stroll the streets of downtown Laguna Beach to find one-of-a-kind jewelry, handcrafted crafts, and art pieces. The Laguna Art Museum's gift store offers one-of-a-kind, art-inspired items and mementos. Don't miss it.

## Accommodation Options in Orange County

Whether you're searching for luxury resorts, boutique hotels or family-friendly lodgings, Orange County offers it all.

**Paséa Hotel and Spa:**
Paséa Hotel & Spa provides a luxury beachfront experience complete with breathtaking ocean views, contemporary facilities, and a soothing spa. This hotel, located only steps from the Huntington Beach Pier, is ideal for travellers looking to stay in the heart of Surf City.

**Kimpton Shorebreak Huntington Beach Resort:**
The Kimpton Shorebreak Huntington Beach Resort is a fantastic option for a stylish and relaxing vacation. This boutique hotel has modern accommodations, a lively social environment, and convenient access to the beach and downtown Huntington Beach's shops and restaurants.

**The Resort at Pelican Hill:**

The Resort at Pelican Hill represents the pinnacle of luxury in Newport Beach. This resort, located on 504 acres of gorgeous beachfront, has Italian-inspired architecture, a world-class golf course, and an exquisite spa. The huge bungalows and villas have stunning ocean views, making it a great destination for a luxurious holiday.

**Balboa Bay Resort:**

This waterfront resort, situated on the picturesque Balboa Bay, combines elegance and comfort. Balboa Bay Resort offers a relaxing and refined stay with waterfront views, expensive dining selections, and a magnificent spa.

**Montage Laguna Beach:**
Montage Laguna Beach, located on a coastal bluff, provides an unrivalled luxury experience with its magnificent beachside setting, outstanding cuisine, and top-tier spa. The resort's craftsman-style buildings and attractively manicured grounds provide a peaceful escape.

**Casa Laguna Hotel and Spa:**

Casa Laguna Hotel & Spa offers a more personal and boutique experience. This ancient home has Spanish-style buildings, gorgeous grounds, and a peaceful spa. It's ideal for people looking for a romantic and relaxing getaway.

From eating and shopping to lodging, Orange County provides a varied and diverse experience that caters to any traveller's needs. Whether you're relishing gourmet meals with ocean views, indulging in retail therapy at premium shopping malls, or relaxing at magnificent beachside resorts, the Pacific Coast Highway through Orange County delivers an unparalleled combination of leisure, adventure, and exploration. Embrace the seaside charm, immerse yourself in the lively local culture, and make memorable memories in this stunning California destination.

# CHAPTER 10

## ORANGE COUNTY TO SAN DIEGO

As the Pacific Coast Highway nears its finish, the lively soul of Southern California comes to life. This journey takes you from the affluent sprawl of Orange County to San Clemente, a place that embodies the traditional California beach town. San Clemente, known for its gorgeous beaches, Spanish Colonial-style architecture, and laid-back ambiance, is a surf and sun-seeker's dream.

**The San Clemente Pier**, a landmark of this coastal community, extends into the Pacific, encouraging tourists to enjoy a leisurely walk across the sea. As waves break against the pylons below, you'll see fishermen casting their lines and residents admiring the breathtaking sunsets that colour the sky in orange, pink, and purple. This is a location where time slows down and the rhythmic sounds of the water provide a soothing backdrop for your thoughts.

San Clemente's central section, Avenida Del Mar, is dotted with attractive stores, cafés, and restaurants. The fragrance of fresh coffee fills the air as you walk by stores offering beachwear, souvenirs, and local art. Don't miss out on the opportunity to have lunch at one of the numerous restaurants serving seaside cuisine. The daily menu includes fresh seafood, crisp salads, and refreshing beverages. For a more relaxing experience, visit one of the many taco stands selling some of the greatest fish tacos you've ever had.

Continuing south gets you to **Oceanside**, a community with a significant military history and a thriving cultural scene. Oceanside, home to **Marine Corps Base Camp Pendleton**, proudly preserves its military origins while providing tourists with a variety of recreational opportunities. The Oceanside Pier, one of the longest wooden piers on the West Coast, is enticed by its magnificent vistas and nostalgic atmosphere. Stroll down the pier, watch surfers ride the waves, and maybe get a snack at the 1950s-style restaurant at the end.

Oceanside's port district is another treasure, with its marina, lovely shops, and waterfront eateries. Renting a kayak or paddleboard is a popular way to enjoy the harbour's quiet waters. The adjacent beaches, such as Harbor Beach and Oceanside Beach, are ideal for sunbathing, swimming, and picnics. The Oceanside Museum of Art, as well as the countless murals that decorate buildings around downtown, highlight the city's lively art culture.

## Explore San Diego:
### *Gaslamp Quarter, Balboa Park, and San Diego Zoo.*

The Pacific Coast Highway adventure concludes at San Diego, a city packed with attractions and rich history. **The Gaslamp Quarter,** in the center of downtown San Diego, is a vibrant neighbourhood that perfectly mixes Victorian-era architecture with contemporary skyscrapers. The Gaslamp Quarter's ancient buildings, gas lighting, and cobblestone streets transport you to another era. This 16-block neighbourhood is home to over 100 restaurants, pubs, and nightclubs, making it the heart of San Diego's nightlife.

During the day, the Gaslamp Quarter has a wealth of activities. Boutiques, galleries, and cafés cover the streets, beckoning you to shop, dine, and enjoy the lively environment. As the sun goes down, the neighbourhood morphs into a vibrant nightlife attraction, with music emanating from clubs, pubs, and rooftop patios. For a one-of-a-kind experience, visit one of the speakeasies concealed behind inconspicuous doors, which serve handmade drinks in an intimate atmosphere.

**Balboa Park,** located only a short drive from the Gaslamp Quarter, is a cultural sanctuary in the center of San Diego. The park spans 1,200 acres and includes 17 museums, magnificent gardens, and the world-famous San Diego Zoo. The park's Spanish-Renaissance architecture, rich landscaping, and peaceful strolling routes make it an ideal spot for relaxation and exploration. The Botanical Building, with its lily pond and exotic plants, is a must-see, as are the breathtaking gardens, such as the Japanese Friendship Garden and the Desert Garden.

Art fans can discover a wealth of exhibitions at the San Diego Museum of Art, the Museum of Photographic Arts, and the Timken Museum of Art, among others. Each museum provides a distinct viewpoint on art, history, and culture, making Balboa Park a paradise for inquisitive minds. The park also has the Old Globe Theatre, where you may see a play in a small, open-air setting evocative of Shakespeare's Globe Theatre in London.

**The San Diego Zoo**, one of the world's biggest and most known zoos, is another must-see attraction for every visitor to San Diego. The zoo, located inside Balboa Park, covers 100 acres and is home to about 3,500 animals representing more than 650 species. The zoo's naturalistic settings and dedication to conservation make it a pioneer in animal care and education. From the lush, tropical environs of the Monkey Trail to the sprawling Elephant

Odyssey, each exhibit provides an insight into the wide world of animals.

The zoo's highlights include the Giant Panda Research Station, where visitors can view these rare and charming species up close, and the Africa Rocks exhibit, which showcases the continent's distinctive fauna and environments. A trip on the Skyfari aerial tram provides a bird's-eye perspective of the zoo and the city beyond.

As you make your way from Orange County to San Diego, it's evident that the Pacific Coast Highway is more than just a road; it's an experience that captures the spirit of California's coastal beauty, dynamic communities, and diverse cultural history. From the lovely beaches of San Clemente to the vibrant streets of the Gaslamp Quarter, each stop adds a new chapter to this remarkable journey.

San Diego is a city that seamlessly mixes the old and contemporary, with ancient monuments standing alongside cutting-edge attractions. The voyage may be coming to an end, but the memories created along the Pacific Coast Highway will endure a lifetime. So, take a minute to enjoy the final rays of the California sun, inhale the salty coastal air, and think about the magnificent adventure that has led you here. The journey may have finished, but the experience has only just begun.

## Best Beaches:
### *(La Jolla and Coronado)*

San Diego's beaches are famous, with two of the best located in La Jolla and Coronado. Each of these coastal treasures has its unique combination of natural beauty, recreational activities, and individual character.

**La Jolla:**

La Jolla, sometimes known as the "Jewel of San Diego," lives up to its reputation with stunning landscape and a refined but relaxing attitude. La Jolla Cove is undoubtedly the most famous location, known for its clean, quiet waters ideal for snorkelling and diving. The underwater marine reserve here is packed with colourful fish, sea lions, and the rare leopard shark, making it a haven for underwater fans.

The cliffs above La Jolla Cove provide breathtaking panoramic views of the Pacific

Ocean. The neighbourhood is studded with grassy parks where you may picnic and enjoy the coastal air. For those who prefer to keep dry, adjacent La Jolla Shores offers a long, sandy beach perfect for sunbathing, surfing, and paddleboarding. The mild waves make it an ideal location for novices beginning to surf.

Beyond the beaches, La Jolla has luxury eating, shopping, and cultural attractions. The Museum of Contemporary Art San Diego, situated directly on the cliffs, has an exceptional collection of modern and contemporary art. La Jolla Village is home to stylish shops, art galleries, and a variety of high-end eateries. Don't pass up the opportunity to eat at one of the beachside restaurants, where you may enjoy exquisite food while watching the sunset over the Pacific.

**Coronado:**

Coronado Island, located just over the renowned Coronado Bridge, seems like a world apart.

Coronado is known for its clean, broad sandy beaches and the historic Hotel del Coronado. It has a lovely, small-town feel with a touch of sophistication. Coronado Beach, frequently named among the greatest in the United States, has dazzling mica in its sand, giving the beach a shimmering appearance.

The Hotel del Coronado, a National Historic Landmark, looms magnificently on the beach. This Victorian-era resort, with its characteristic red-roofed turrets, has been a favoured getaway for celebrities, presidents, and kings since its inception in 1888. Even if you don't stay at the hotel, it's worth stopping by to appreciate the architecture, eat, or have a glass on the beachside terrace.

Orange Avenue, Coronado's main thoroughfare, is dotted with quaint boutiques, cafés, and restaurants. The island's laidback, pedestrian-friendly vibe is ideal for a leisurely walk or bike ride. Rent a bike and explore the picturesque paths, or visit the Coronado Ferry

Landing for spectacular views of San Diego's skyline.

**Dining and Accommodations in San Diego**

San Diego's culinary culture is as varied and dynamic as the city itself. Whether you want fresh seafood, genuine Mexican cuisine, or creative farm-to-table meals, you'll find them here.

Dining:

Begin your gastronomic excursion in Little Italy, a vibrant district noted for its superb Italian restaurants, artisan breweries, and contemporary cafés. Enjoy homemade pasta and wood-fired pizzas at one of the several trattorias, or try fresh seafood at the Little Italy Mercato Farmers' Market, which is held every Saturday.

Visit **Old Town** to experience San Diego's Mexican history. This historic district is considered the birthplace of California, and its streets are lined with eateries providing traditional Mexican cuisine. Enjoy enchiladas, tamales, and margaritas in a vibrant, festive setting. Many of the restaurants have live mariachi music, which adds to the dynamic atmosphere.

The Gaslamp Quarter has an unusual mix of eating choices, ranging from luxury steakhouses to contemporary tapas eateries. Rooftop pubs and restaurants provide spectacular views of the city skyline, ideal for a romantic supper or a night out with friends. For a one-of-a-kind eating experience, stop into one of the numerous speakeasies concealed around the neighbourhood, where artisan drinks and gourmet snacks await.

La Jolla and Coronado also provide a diverse range of eating alternatives, from informal coastal cafés to upscale dining venues. George's at the Cove in La Jolla serves fresh seafood and has a patio with breathtaking views of the ocean. In Coronado, **Del's 1500 OCEAN** restaurant offers an exceptional dining experience with farm-to-table food and panoramic ocean views.

## Accommodation

San Diego has a broad choice of lodgings to meet any traveller's requirements, from luxurious resorts to low-cost motels and beautiful bed & breakfasts.

Several boutique hotels in the Gaslamp Quarter provide contemporary facilities while retaining their historic charm. The Pendry San Diego, for example, combines modern flair with traditional elegance, with a rooftop pool and a variety of dining choices.

**The Hotel del Coronado** is a good option for a beachside stay. This landmark resort provides a variety of accommodations, including magnificent beachside cottages and old Victorian rooms. The resort offers many restaurants, a spa, and a range of leisure activities.

The **La Valencia Hotel** in La Jolla, often known as the "Pink Lady," combines Mediterranean-style grandeur with breathtaking coastal views. This ancient hotel has magnificent suites, a stunning pool area, and a well-known restaurant.

If you prefer a more private setting, San Diego boasts several delightful bed & breakfasts and boutique inns. The Keating House, situated in the Banker's Hill district, has Victorian-style rooms and a warm, inviting ambiance.

For budget-conscious tourists, there are several economical alternatives across the city, including well-known brands and independent hotels. The Old Town Inn, situated in Old Town, offers pleasant rooms at a fair price and convenient access to many of San Diego's major attractions.

As your trip along the Pacific Coast Highway comes to an end in San Diego, you'll be left with a tapestry of memories woven from the different experiences and stunning views of the California coast. From the peaceful beaches of San Clemente and Oceanside to the lively cultural hotspots of the Gaslamp Quarter and Balboa Park, each stop along the route has lent its distinct flavour to this amazing journey.

San Diego provides a finishing flourish, combining natural beauty, historical history, and a vibrant metropolitan landscape. Whether you're exploring the upmarket appeal of La Jolla, the timeless elegance of Coronado, or the vibrant heart of downtown, the city encourages you to immerse yourself in its many pleasures.

The Pacific Coast Highway is more than simply a route; it is an experience that encapsulates the essence of California. It's a location where the trip is just as spectacular as the goal. So, when you say goodbye to the winding roads and coastal panoramas, realize that the memories and experiences you've gained will remain with you, inspiring future adventures and rekindling the charm of the California coast whenever you need them.

Safe travels!

# CHAPTER 11
## MAPS

# MONTEREY

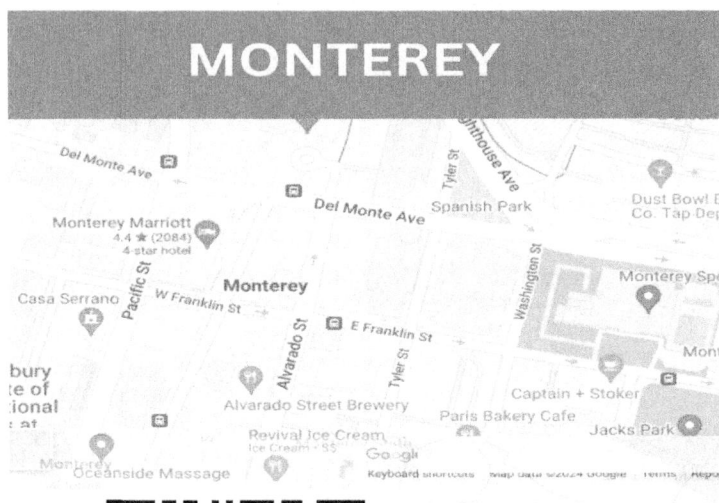

Scan me

### How to use this map
1. Open the camera app on your device.
2. Point the camera at the QR code until a notification appears.
3. Tap the notification to open the link.
4. Select "Open in Maps" or your preferred mapping app.
5. The map will display the location and provide directions.

# Hearst Castle

Neptune Pool

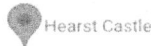
Hearst Castle

Google
Keyboard shortcuts

**How to use this map**
1. Open the camera app on your device.
2. Point the camera at the QR code until a notification appears.
3. Tap the notification to open the link.
4. Select "Open in Maps" or your preferred mapping app.
5. The map will display the location and provide directions.

## Scan me

191

# Camel by-the-sea

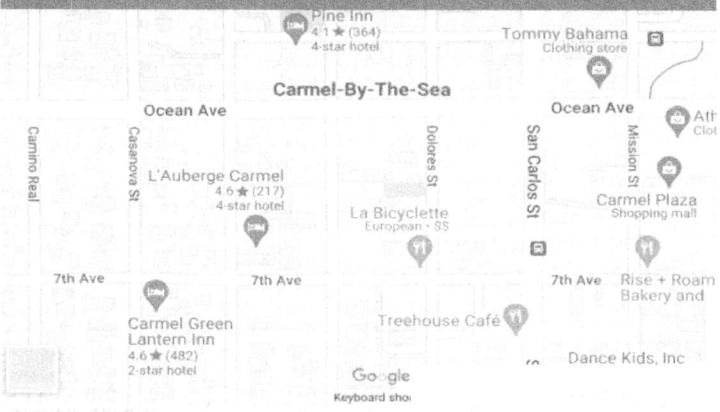

Scan me

### How to use this map

1. Open the camera app on your device.
2. Point the camera at the QR code until a notification appears.
3. Tap the notification to open the link.
4. Select "Open in Maps" or your preferred mapping app.
5. The map will display the location and provide directions.

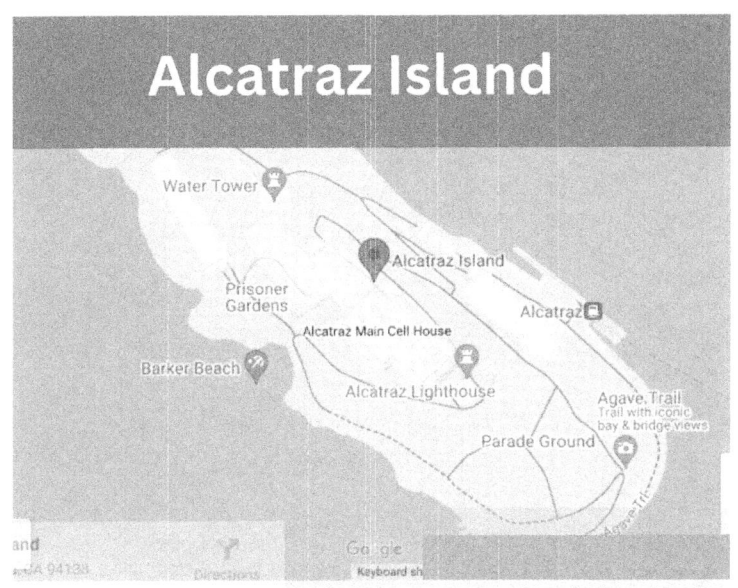

### How to use this map

1. Open the camera app on your device.
2. Point the camera at the QR code until a notification appears.
3. Tap the notification to open the link.
4. Select "Open in Maps" or your preferred mapping app.
5. The map will display the location and provide directions.

193

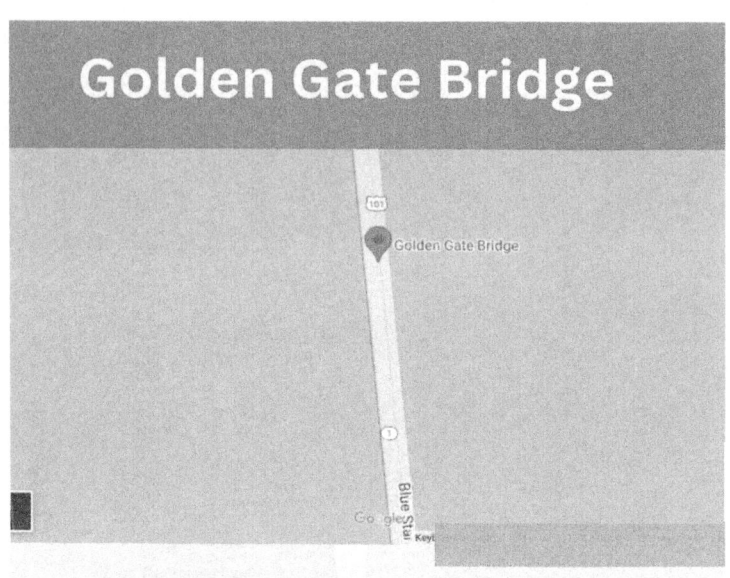

**How to use this map**
1. Open the camera app on your device.
2. Point the camera at the QR code until a notification appears.
3. Tap the notification to open the link.
4. Select "Open in Maps" or your preferred mapping app.
5. The map will display the location and provide directions.

### How to use this map

1. Open the camera app on your device.
2. Point the camera at the QR code until a notification appears.
3. Tap the notification to open the link.
4. Select "Open in Maps" or your preferred mapping app.
5. The map will display the location and provide directions.

## Scan me

Printed in Great Britain
by Amazon